Krishna's Mercy

1

Maintainer of the Universe

Daily articles from August 2009

Equality

"Different living entities appear in different forms of dress, but according to the instruction of the Bhagavad-gita, a learned person sees all living entities equally. Such treatment by the devotee is very much appreciated by the Supreme Lord." (Shrila Prabhupada, Shrimad Bhagavatam, 4.11.13 Purport)

The recent election of Barrack Obama to the presidency of the United States was regarded worldwide as a landmark occasion. American has officially been a country for over two hundred years, but this was the first time in its history that a person of color, an Africa-American, was elected as president. Many thought that this day would never come, for they viewed America as a racist country. Yet, one is left to wonder whether Obama's election was really that groundbreaking.

Black people have not been treated very well historically in America. During the country's founding, most blacks weren't even treated as human beings, but rather were slaves, owned and traded as property. The founding fathers struggled very hard with the issue of slavery while adopting the Constitution, eventually tabling the issue, allowing the process to continue. Slowly but surely however, slavery would meet its end, culminating with the Civil War during the early 1860s. However, even after the abolition of slavery, blacks were still discriminated against, especially in the Southern portion of the country, where they would periodically be lynched or harassed in other ways. This treatment continued for almost one hundred years, until the Civil Rights movement of the late 1960s. Due to this history of racism, many blacks felt that the country was forever doomed and incapable of electing a black person to any meaningful position of power. The election of Obama was redemption for them, offering a glimmer of hope that maybe people no longer made judgments about others based on their ethnicity or skin color.

On the surface it appears that progress has been made, but according to the Vedic teachings, it hasn't. The central tenet of any religion, but especially the Vedas, is that we are not our bodies. One may then ask, "Well, if we are not our bodies, then what are we?" The answer in Sanskrit is *aham brahmasmi*, "I am a spirit soul". Our souls are certainly enclosed inside of our bodies, but this body is constantly changing. The body we had as a child is completely different from the one we have as adults, yet we don't mourn for the death of our childhood. In the same manner, a wise person doesn't lament over the death of the current body, which is nothing more than clothing that is given up at the time of death and then replaced again in our next birth.

"As a person puts on new garments, giving up old ones, similarly, the soul accepts new material bodies, giving up the old and useless ones." (Lord Krishna, Bhagavad-gita, 2.22)

Since most of us aren't taught about the soul in school, we are falsely identifying with the body. Though it may be nice that a black person has been elected president, constitutionally such a person is no different than all the others who previously held the esteemed title of President of the United States. Sure their life experiences may have all been different, some enduring more discrimination growing up than others, but that is something we all deal with. The material world means a place full of miseries, *dukhalayam*. Every living entity is forced to suffer the fourfold miseries of life: birth, old age, disease, and death.

The Vedas declare that anyone who identifies with the gross material body is a *mudha*, or an ass. An animal has little to no intelligence, and is certainly not smart enough to understand the concept of the soul and changing bodies. The human being is unique in its ability to take in this information and use it for its benefit. However, if we continue to identify ourselves as black, white, man, woman, American, etc., then our intelligence is very limited. Real progress comes when we view everyone equally, as a spirit soul part and parcel of the Supreme Personality of Godhead, Lord Krishna.

"The Blessed Lord said: He who does not hate illumination, attachment and delusion when they are present, nor longs for them when they disappear; who is seated like one unconcerned, being situated beyond these material reactions of the modes of nature, who remains firm, knowing that the modes alone are active; who regards alike pleasure and pain, and looks on a clod, a stone and a piece of gold with an equal eye; who is wise and holds praise and blame to be the same; who is unchanged in honor and dishonor, who treats friend and foe alike, who has abandoned all fruitive undertakings-such a man is said to have transcended the modes of nature." (Lord Krishna, Bhagavad-gita, 14.22)

Since most people live on the material platform, the Vedas give different directions on how material life should be governed. They state that society should be divided into four classes based off of one's qualities. Also, the time span of one's life should also be divided into four stages or *ashramas*, each progressively leading one to spiritual perfection. This system, known as *varnashrama dharma*, is the code for managing society with the aim of helping everyone progress spiritually. So in this system, there are material designations such as those between men and women, brahmanas, shudras, vaishyas, etc. These are all material, but one can rise above them immediately by becoming a devotee of Krishna. The bhaktas, or devotees, are above any material designation. Since they have a pure love for Krishna, they are *mahajanas*, or completely spiritual beings following the original principles of religion.

Many examples of this fact can be found in the Vedas. When God came to earth as the pious prince Lord Rama, He wandered through the forest for fourteen years as an exile with His wife Sita and younger brother Lakshmana. During that time, the Treta Yuga, the varnashrama dharma system was adhered to, and those living in the forest were generally viewed as lower class living entities. Basically anyone not living in a normal house, except for the brahmanas, was considered uncivilized. Early on in His travels, the Lord and His family met the Nishada chief Guha. The Nishadas were a tribe living in the forests that were generally viewed as outcastes. However, Guha showed great hospitality to Rama and His family, and for this the Lord gave Him His blessings. Guha was a pure devotee and was rewarded with the opportunity to personally offer food and hospitality to God Himself. His caste was completely meaningless, for God viewed Him very favorably.

Later on, in another incident, the Lord teamed up with the Vanara king Sugriva. Vanaras were a race of monkeys with human-like characteristics. Rama helped Sugriva regain his lost kingdom by killing his brother Vali. Sugriva was very distraught after his brother's death, and he blamed himself for what he viewed as a horrible deed. Bewailing thus, Sugriva begged forgiveness from Rama, stating that he was just a lowly monkey with very little intelligence. Now Sugriva was a great devotee, so he was by no means unintelligent, but he was referencing a generality that existed at the time. Since they were more monkey-like than human-like, the Vanaras were especially known for their animalistic tendencies, with one of them being their penchant for getting drunk off a certain type of honey. Yet again, God overlooked these stereotypes and looked at what was in Sugriva's heart. As pure devotees, Sugriva and his Vanara army were given the opportunity to directly serve the Lord by helping Him battle Ravana and rescue Sita. The greatest of the Vanara warriors was Hanuman, Sugriva's chief deputy. Considered Lord Rama's greatest devotee, Hanuman is above is all material designations. He is completely spiritual, a great soul with immense strength, able to assume any shape at will. He uses his strength only to serve the Lord and for this reason he is still celebrated today.

To serve Lord Krishna properly, Lord Chaitanya recommended everyone to follow the mode of worship subscribed to by the gopis of Vrindavana. When the Lord personally came to earth around five thousand years ago, He spent His youth in Vrindavana as a cowherd boy, the son of His foster parents Nanda and Yashoda. The gopis, the cowherd girls of Vrindavana, were completely in love with Krishna, and they spent all their time thinking of Him. They weren't high class yogis or Vedantists. They even openly declared themselves to be unintelligent, for women didn't receive a formal education during those times. However, their pure devotion actually made them smarter than the greatest of scholars. Many of us go to God with some personal motive, either we want something or we want relief from some ailment. The gopis however just wanted to always be with Krishna, and to always love Him. This is the highest form of worship, and for this reason Krishna is eternally associated with His gopis, the greatest of them being Shrimati Radharani.

The lesson here is that if we want to make real progress as a society, then we should all become Krishna conscious. That will immediately afford us the opportunity to break free of all material designations. Though the performance of great Vedic sacrifices requires an expert brahmanas or priest, the process of devotional service is open to anyone.

"O son of Partha, those who take shelter in Me, though they be of lower birth-women, vaishyas [merchants], as well as shudras [workers]—can approach the supreme destination." (Lord Krishna, Bhagavad-gita, 9.32)

Knowing this fact, we should all take up bhakti yoga, for that is the only path taken by all the great souls.

A Perfect Sannyasi

"I shall wend my way to the forest impassable, devoid of men, inhabited by various deer, tigers, and other voracious animals." (Sita Devi speaking to Lord Rama, Valmiki Ramayana, Ayodhya Kand, Sec 27)

The Vedic texts often make reference to forest life or one's living in a forest. Similar to the modern day concept of homelessness, having to live in the forest means living without any material comforts. The forest is meant for wild animals, birds, and other beasts, and not for human beings. Even in the modern age, many people go camping in the woods to get a taste for the wilderness. It is considered "roughing it" to live without electricity, having to procure food and shelter for oneself. Even heat must be generated through one's own efforts by starting fires and keeping them burning. These camping trips are usually short in duration; lasting no more than a few days, for living in the woods is no easy task. The amenities available to us in urban life such as toilet paper and hot water are hard to come by when one is out enjoying nature.

On the other hand, the forest is devoid of human beings, so it is considered a place of great solitude. According to Vedic philosophy, one isn't supposed to remain in family life all the way until death. For men, life is divided into four stages, known as *ashramas*. The fours *ashramas* are bramhacharya, grihastha, vanaprastha, and sannyasya. Brahmacharya refers to celibate student life where one takes instruction from his guru and learns the art of serving Krishna, or God. Grihastha is the mode of life where one lives with a wife, produces offspring, and earns a living. Vanaprastha is the time of retired family life where one stops fruitive work and concentrates on serving God, and if often involves travelling to holy places with one's wife. Sannyasa is the final stage of life and it involves complete renunciation from family life and fruitive work. God made this the last stage in one's spiritual progression because this is the time when one prepares to die.

According to the Bhagavad-gita, if one thinks of Krishna at the time of death, then they are guaranteed never to return to this material world.

"And whoever, at the time of death, quits his body, remembering Me alone, at once attains My nature. Of this there is no doubt." (Lord Krishna, Bhagavad-gita, 8.5)

Sannyasa is the time for one to seriously practice thinking of Krishna and become completely dependent on Him for everything. There are many rules and regulations associated with being a sannyasi, but the most important is that one must not have any intimate connection with women. Sex life is the biggest hindrance to spiritual understanding, so it is sanctioned for grihasthis, but not for people in any of the other three ashramas. Even a grihasthi is to abide by many rules and regulations when engaging in sex life, such as only having sex for procreation. This means that married couples should only have intimate relations during the wife's fertile period of the month, and then only after adhering to the *garbhadhana-samskara*.

"When the mentality of the father and mother is completely Krishna consciousness, so that when there will be sexual intercourse, the mentality of the child will be Krishna conscious. This is the *garbhadhana-samskara*." (Shrila Prabhupada, Lecture, 731229SB.LA)

Samskaras are rites or reformatory processes which people should adhere to if possible, for it will help them to make spiritual progress.

In order to be free from family attachments, during Vedic times, sannyasis would leave home and live in the forest. Forest life isn't fit for normal people, but for one who is completely renounced and has his mind fixed on Krishna. For them, the forest is one of the most pleasing places to live.

When Lord Krishna appeared on this earth in His avatar of Lord Rama, He was exiled to live in the forest for fourteen years by His father, Maharaja Dashratha, the king of Ayodhya. Now Lord Rama was God Himself, the ultimate renunciate, so He had no problem accepting this decree. One is known as God when He possesses all six opulences of life in full and simultaneously. Krishna is the most famous, the most beautiful, the richest, the wisest, the most powerful, and the greatest renunciate. Upon being given this order by His father, Lord Rama went to inform His wife Sita of the bad news. The Lord instructed her to remain at home for the exile period, where she would be protected. Sita Devi vehemently protested His request and put forth a series of counter arguments in hopes of persuading the Lord to allow her to come with Him. The forest is very dangerous for human beings, so Sita made sure to inform the Lord that she knew exactly what to expect. She had no reservations about going with the Lord.

Far from being a typical sannyasi, Sita was the most beautiful woman who grew up as a princess. Living in the royal court of King Janaka, and then as the daughter-in-law of King Dashratha, she was accustomed to having every material comfort at her disposal. It was for this reason that everyone was worried about how she would survive forest life. With this being the case, how and why was she so eager to follow her husband and live a life tailored for great renunciates? The answer is that Sita was completely devoted to Lord Rama, God Himself. When one is perfectly practicing devotional service, known as bhakti yoga, then he or she has no attachments to anything material. Such a person is actually a complete renunciate and thus a perfect sannyasi. So though there may be many rules and regulations as part of the varnashrama dharma system, we see that one can transcend all those rules instantly by becoming a devotee of the Lord. God is very nice to us in this age because He incarnates through His holy name. We should learn to accept His mercy by constantly chanting His holy name in a loving manner. Doing so will make us the perfect sannyasis, capable of enduring any and all hardships.

Gopi Jana Vallabha

13

"Gopi-jana vallabha, Giri-vara-dhari" (Shrila Bhaktivinoda Thakura)

This is a line from the poem called *Jaya Radha Madhava*, composed by Shrila Bhaktivinoda Thakura, a great saint in the line of spiritual masters descending from Lord Chaitanya. Glorifying Lord Krishna and His principle devotees, this poem, turned into a song, was made famous throughout the world by His Divine Grace A.C. Bhaktivedanta Swami Prabhupada and today is sung daily in hundreds of temple throughout the world.

Lord Krishna is the sustainer of the gopis. Around five thousand years ago, the Lord personally advented on this planet and spent His childhood in Vrindavana, a town in India. There are three primary forms of God which are interchangeable: Krishna, Narayana, and Vishnu. They are the same one and only God, above any other demigod, but according to the Shrimad Bhagavatam and other major Vedic texts, Krishna is the original. It is similar to the concept of a single candle lighting many others. All other candles are the same in their potency, but the original candle still stands out. Krishna's expansions are known as *vishnu-tattva*. His incarnations as Rama, Narasimha, Vamana, etc. are all as good as God Himself. In essence when discussing and comparing His various names and forms and their various potencies, it's really a matter of a distinction without a difference. When Krishna came to earth, it was in His original form, and He came to give protection to His devotees, to kill the demons, and to enact pastimes for future generations to relish in.

The gopis were the cowherd girls of Vrindavana. Krishna spent His childhood living in a vaishya family. Vaishyas are the third division or caste of society and their duty is to run businesses and engage in cow protection. Nanda Maharaja, Krishna's foster father, was a cowherd man as were the rest of the inhabitants of Vrindavana. The gopis were mostly married girls who worked all day as milkmaids and who managed household affairs. Most of them were married but they still spent all their time thinking about Krishna and His welfare. He was their life and soul. This is the mood of a pure devotee. We may have family ties and friendships during our lifetime, but our eternal relationship with God trumps all others. He is the only reservoir of pleasure, and those who realize this fact have made their lives perfect. As a child, Krishna and His friends would go out and play or they would take the cows out to the pastures, and the gopis would worry all day about Him. "How is Krishna doing? Is He alright? Is He having fun? When He comes home, we will serve Him nice food and make Him happy." In this way, their minds were completely fixed on the Supreme Lord in perfect meditation like perfect yogis. They obviously weren't yogis, for they were uneducated girls, but through their service, their activities were better than that of any yogi. There are 108 primary gopis, and for this reason the japa mala, or set of chanting beads, has 108 beads on them with an additional primary bead representing Krishna. If one thinks of the gopis while chanting on these beads, then he or she will gradually be elevated to the state of pure Krishna consciousness.

The gopis in Vrindavana actually descended from the spiritual world. The kingdom of God has many spiritual planets, with the primary one being Krishnaloka. Vrindavana actually exists there in its original form, and the same pastimes are occurring their eternally. The gopis that took birth in Vrindavana did so to as to allow the same pastimes to occur on earth for others to see and hear about. Many of the gopis were also great sages in their previous lives, during the advent of Lord Rama.

"The gopis who were gathered there were mostly all followers of the Vedas. In their previous births, during Lord Ramachandra's advent, they were Vedic scholars who desired the association of Lord Ramachandra in conjugal love. Ramachandra gave them the benediction that they would be present for the advent of Lord Krishna, and He would fulfill their desires. During Krishna's advent, the Vedic scholars took birth in the shape of the gopis in Vrndavana; as young gopis, they got the association of Krishna in fulfillment of their previous births' desire. The ultimate goal of their perfect desire was attained, and they were so joyous that they had nothing further to desire." (Krsna, The Supreme Personality of Godhead, 1970-1-31)

Lord Rama lived by the principle of *eka-patni*, having only one wife in Sita Devi. Being God Himself, He was highly sought after by many others, but He didn't want to break His vow, so He accommodated those people by allowing them to take birth in the future where they could have association with Him.

The gopis didn't look for pleasure from material things. We all tend to seek after the material comforts of a nice home, money, a nice husband or wife, and good children. These certainly aren't bad things, for they provide security and happiness. However, that is not ultimate aim of life. Family relations and money are nonetheless temporary, for one has to give them up at the time of death. If one wants permanent happiness, they need only look to God. The gopis didn't pray for anything material, for they only wanted Krishna to be happy. They were the greatest renunciates without even knowing it. Most of us initially approach God for some personal benefit. One of our friends or family members may be suffering from an illness, so we pray to God to cure their ailment. Other times we may fall victim to some bad luck, and we pray to God to lift us out of our difficult situations. This type of worship certainly isn't bad, for at least we realize that there is a God, a higher power who has greater control over things than we do. At the same time, God is not our order supplier. Everything that happens in this material world is a result of the laws of nature and karma. If we ask God for something and He doesn't give it to us, that doesn't mean He doesn't exist. The dualities of happiness and distress, good and bad fortune all come and go of their own volition without us seeking them. Our real business is to love God for who He is and not for what He can supply us.

Jaya Radha Madhava is a very nice song to sing, for it puts us in a good place. We can immediately think of the beauty of Vrindavana and the wonderful pastimes that occur there. Following in the path of the gopis, we can do no wrong.

Life Is Meant For Austerity

"Then raising the vessel of ghee (clarified butter) to His head, He in accordance with the ordinance began to offer oblations to the flaming fire on behalf of the mighty deity. Then, having partaken of the remaining quanity of the ghee, Rama prayed for His own welfare, and meditated on Narayana. The son of the best of men with a collected mind, and restraining His speech lay down on a kusha (grass) bed together with Vaidehi (Sita) within the graceful dwelling of Vishnu." (Valmiki Ramayana, Ayodhya Kanda, Sec 6)

We live in an era of great comfort and luxury. Though people may think otherwise, the standard of living in America, and throughout the world for that matter, has greatly improved over the past hundred years. The economic problem is almost non-existent, with farmers persuaded by the government to not grow food. Our leaders are more focused on tackling *problems* such as childhood obesity and the perceived overconsumption of goods and services by the population in general.

When travelling on commercial airplanes, one of the magazines commonly found in the seatback pocket is *Sky Mall*. This magazine is a shopping catalog full of gadgets and gizmos, a showcase of the latest advancements in technology. All the products in that magazine are geared towards gratifying our senses. One place where we often look for improved sense gratification is in the area of sleep. Ironically, the Vedas prescribe that one shouldn't sleep more than six hours if possible. This is in stark contrast to the eight hours prescribed by most health experts.

"One should not sleep more than six hours daily. One who sleeps more than six hours out of twenty-four is certainly influenced by the mode of ignorance. A person in the mode of ignorance is lazy and prone to sleep a great deal. Such a person cannot perform yoga." (Shrila Prabhupada, Bhagavad-gita, 6.16 Purport)

Since we spend so much time sleeping, naturally we are looking for ways to increase the quality of it. Products such as the *Sleep Number Bed* from *Select Comfort* allow couples to set different firmness levels on their mattress so that each person can spend the night in the utmost comfort. In addition, regular blankets apparently aren't good enough for us, so we shop for luxury items such as down comforters. Water beds are another popular phenomenon in the mattress industry.

These products are no doubt very innovative and could certainly prove to be useful. However, they don't provide us real happiness in the end. If they did, then there would be no need for new products to come out. The fact of the matter is that our real problems have nothing to do with our material comforts. According to wisdom of the Vedas, man's material sense urges can never be satisfied. Making little adjustments here and there to our material condition only further binds us in the mode of passion.

"My dear Uddhava, a person bereft of intelligence first falsely identifies himself with the material body and mind, and when such false knowledge arises within one's consciousness, material passion, the cause of great suffering, pervades the mind, which by nature is situated in goodness. Then the mind, contaminated by passion, becomes absorbed in making and changing many plans for material advancement. Thus, by constantly thinking of the modes of material nature, a foolish person is afflicted with unbearable material desires." (Lord Krishna, Shrimad Bhagavatam, 11.13.9-10)

We get a new bed, but then we immediately want a better blanket. We get a new blanket, but then we immediately want new pajamas, and so on. The cycle never ends.

The Vedas tell us that this life is meant for understanding Sleep God. To understand God, one must perform austerities, known as *tapasya*. *Tapasya* is not any ordinary type of austerity, but it is geared towards releasing one from their bondage to material comforts, and thereby increasing their attachment to the spiritual world.

"Lord Rishabhadeva told His sons: My dear boys, of all the living entities who have accepted material bodies in this world, one who has been awarded this human form should not work hard day and night simply for sense gratification, which is available even for dogs and hogs that eat stool. One should engage in penance and austerity to attain the divine position of devotional service. By such activity, one's heart is purified, and when one attains this position, he attains eternal, blissful life, which is transcendental to material happiness and which continues forever." (Shrimad Bhagavatam, 5.5.1)

When Lord Rama was living in the kingdom of Ayodhya, His father, Maharaja Dashratha one day decided to install Him as the new king. Lord Rama was informed of this news one day before the date set for His installation. He was instructed by the brahmanas, the priestly class of men, to fast the night before the ceremony and to sleep on the floor on a bed of *kusha* grass. Rama was God Himself, but He willingly followed the advice of the brahmanas to set a good example for all of us. Religious rituals may seem to strange to us at first, but they all have a purpose.

Rama was the king's eldest and most cherished son, so He was living in complete luxury. What need did he have to sleep on the floor? Yet He and His wife Sita both did so as a means of respecting God. When we receive good benedictions, it is incumbent upon us to remember that we are not the doers. All our fortunes are tied to God and to our karma. Narayana is God's four-handed form existing in the spiritual world. Lord Rama was an incarnation of God, so He went along and worshiped Narayana, though in essence He was offering obeisances to Himself. By worshiping Narayana, the sleeping area was sanctified.

Now things wouldn't go as planned the next day and Rama's installation would have to be postponed by fourteen years, but that didn't make a difference. The Lord was always committed to dharma, not for His sake, but because it serves as a guide for enabling one to make spiritual progress. *Tapasya* properly performed under the direction of a spiritual master never goes to waste. Through good times and bad, we must always remember the Creator. God showed us the proper means of penance and it is important for us to follow His example. The most basic form of penance we can perform is to abstain from the four pillars of sinful life: meat eating, illicit sex, gambling, and intoxication. By so doing, we will always remember God and be freed from our material attachments.

Brotherly Love

23

"Even from early youth, that enhancer of auspiciousness, Lakshmana, was ever attached to his eldest brother Rama, that delight of all. Like to another life of Rama, Lakshmana furnished with auspiciousness was in everything attentive to Rama's wishes, even at the neglect of his own person. That foremost of persons did not even attain sleep without Rama's company, nor did he partake of any sweetmeat that was offered, unless Rama partook of it with him." (Valmiki Ramayana, Bala Kand)

There is nothing like having a brother, someone with whom an immediate bond can be formed. A brother is someone that we can automatically love without having to think about it. Lakshmana, an incarnation of Lord Baladeva (Lord Krishna's immediate expansion), was the younger brother of Lord Rama and His dearmost friend.

According to the Vedas, God is one even though He has many names and forms. The original form of God is Krishna, who is also known as Vasudeva. Vasudeva's immediate expansion is Sankarshana or Baladeva. Baladeva has other expansions as well, the most notable one being Ananta Shesha Naga, whom all the planets in the universe rest upon. Krishna's four-handed form of Narayana resides on the island of Shvetadvipa, where He lays down upon Shesha Naga while being served and worshiped by Goddess Lakshmi. When the Lord incarnates on earth, Baladeva and Lakshmi usually come with Him.

"Baladeva, Lakshmana, Advaita Acharya, Lord Nityananda, Lord Shesha and Lord Sankarshana taste the nectarean mellows of the transcendental bliss of Lord Krishna by recognizing Themselves as being His devotees and servants. They are all mad with that happiness, and they know nothing else." (Chaitanya Charitamrita, Adi 6.105-106)

When Krishna appeared on earth around five thousand years ago, Baladeva also took birth as His elder brother Balarama. Around five hundred years ago, the same Baladeva appeared in the form of Nityananda Prabhu, Lord Chaitanya's most beloved God brother. When Vasudeva incarnated as Lord Rama many thousands of years ago in Ayodhya, Baladeva took birth as His half-brother Lakshmana. Rama had two other brothers, but Lakshmana was the one with whom He spent the most time. In fact, it can be assumed that throughout His entire time on earth, no one spent more time with Rama than Lakshmana did.

We sometimes see that brothers can get into arguments and fights over issues of jealously and attention from their parents. Known as sibling rivalries, an older brother can sometimes get jealous at the preferential treatment that the younger brother receives. The younger brother can become resentful of the authority that the older brother wields. Sometimes the older brother can get annoyed at having the younger brother tag along with him wherever he goes. The eldest brother or sister is the leader, the one who sets the example for the other siblings. Parents invest greater responsibility in the eldest, so that naturally can get in the way of the friendships formed with younger siblings.

There was no such fighting between Rama and Lakshmana. Lakshmana was attached to Rama from birth and would always follow his elder brother around. He worshiped Him like a father and would never leave His side. Usually younger siblings require more attention from their parents. The young ones are often referred to as the *babies* of the family, and they require the protection and assistance of their elder siblings. In Lakshmana's case, he always looked to protect Rama first. He would think to himself, "Rama is too nice. He doesn't see that others are taking advantage of His kindness. It is my duty to always protect Him and look out for His best interests."

When Lord Rama was banished to the forest for fourteen years by His step-mother Kaikeyi and His father Dashratha, Lakshmana insisted on going with Him. Lakshmana's mother, Sumitra, tried to dissuade her son by telling him that it was his duty to stay and protect his father in the absence of Rama. Lakshmana replied, "Devotion to Rama is the highest dharma for any man. To always serve my elder brother is the only duty that I know of." Early on in their exile, Sita, Rama and Lakshmana were visited in the forest by Bharata and Shatrughna, Rama and Lakshmana's two other brothers, who tried to convince Rama to return to the kingdom. Upon first seeing them, Lakshmana thought maybe the two brothers had come to attack Rama, so he immediately went on guard to protect his brother. Now this wasn't necessary since Bharata and Shatrughna were pure devotees of Rama as well, but it illustrated Lakshmana's devotion to Rama.

While dwelling in the forest, Lakshmana would keep vigil at night while Rama and His wife Sita were sleeping. When traversing the wilderness, Rama would walk in the front and Lakshmana in the back, with Sita in the middle. This way, Lakshmana made sure to protect Rama's wife, whom he treated as his own mother.

Lakshmana was often quick tempered and would go outside the bounds of propriety in defending His brother. Lord Rama excused this from him because He knew that it was done out of love. Sometimes our devotion may not be perfect but God is so merciful. In whatever we do, He always takes into account our love for Him.

Lord Rama was God Himself, so He required no protection whatsoever. Nevertheless, Lakshmana showed us the proper way to serve the Lord. We generally like to ask God for things. "Please let me have this. Please let me have that. Please take away my pain." While that is an acceptable form of worship, since it involves focusing the mind on God, it is still second class. The first class form of worship is the one shown by Lakshmana. "God, how may I serve you? You are too nice to me and to everyone else. Yet still people do not become Your devotees. I will serve You with all my thoughts, words, and deeds. I will protect Your good name."

The highest form of worship is to become God's devotee and to always try to protect Him. In this age of Kali, people are constantly trying to rewrite history and give their own atheistic interpretations of the great Vedic scriptures. They are saying that God is dead, or that God is impersonal and that we are all God. It is up to the bhaktas, the devotees, to protect God's good name from these attacks by teaching others the real meaning of the Vedas. God doesn't require this service from us, but He loves us for our sincerity and our concern, the same way He loves Lakshmana.

Illicit Sex

"(Men in the Kali Yuga) behave contrary to the modes of life to which they betake themselves. They are addicted to consuming intoxicating drinks and their unfettered sexual desires make them capable of even coveting the wife of their guru. Their desires are all on the material platform." (Markandeya Rishi speaking to King Yudhishthira, Mahabharata, Vana Parva)

This statement is part of a conversation between the venerable Markandeya Rishi and the five Pandava brothers along with their cousin Lord Krishna, the Supreme Personality of Godhead. The epic Mahabharata describes the plight of the brothers to regain their kingdom, detailing the many trials and tribulations they endured while travelling across India around five thousand years ago. Along the way, they took instruction from many great sages, with Markandeya being one of them. In this instance, the sage is acting as spiritual master to the five brothers, headed by King Yudhishthira, describing to them the defects of Kali Yuga.

According to the Vedas, each creation is divided into four time periods or Yugas. Dharma, or religiosity, declines amongst the population by one quarter with each successive Yuga. Kali Yuga, the age we are are currently in, is the fourth and final time period where dharma is notable by its absence. Existing at only one quarter its full strength, most of society today is dedicated to *adharma*, sinful life. It is an evolution of sorts, but not of the Darwinian variety. Instead of the species evolving, it is man's penchant for sinful activity that has gradually evolved and gained in strength. When man first inhabited the earth, he was almost completely pure. The first age is known as Satya or Krita Yuga, meaning the age of truth. Most people were truthful and honest during that time. Gradually however, due to contamination caused by contact with this material world, mankind increased its propensity for sinful activity, to the point now where most are encouraged to act in ways that are completely against the injunctions of the scriptures.

Of all the various types of sins, illicit sex life is considered the greatest. People have many definitions of what exactly constitutes a sin, but the Vedas tell us that sinful activity is anything which causes us to be bound to the repeated cycle of birth and death. Our souls are eternal, but our material bodies are not. At the time of death, we give up our current bodies and get a new one according to our karma. Our current life is not the first one that we've had. This is confirmed by Lord Krishna in the Bhagavad-gita.

"The Blessed Lord said: Many, many births both you (Arjuna) and I have passed. I can remember all of them, but you cannot, O subduer of the enemy!" (Bhagavad-gita, 4.5)

If we are pious, then we take birth in a high family in our next life, and if we are overly sinful, we take birth in a lower family or species. This cycle can be stopped however, by those who really want out of this material world. God actually is very kind to us and gives us exactly what we want. If we want to constantly enjoy unending sex life, He obliges by giving us the body of a dog or a monkey. If we want to be very pious and intelligent, he gives us the body of a great scholar or yogi. By the same token, if we want eternal association with God as His servant, then He obliges by permanently removing us from this material world. If one thinks of Krishna at the time of death, then he or she no longer takes birth in this material world.

"And whoever, at the time of death, quits his body, remembering Me alone, at once attains My nature. Of this there is no doubt. Whatever state of being one remembers when he quits his body, that state he will attain without fail... That abode of Mine is not illumined by the sun or moon, nor by electricity. One who reaches it *never* returns to this material world." (Lord Krishna, Bhagavad-gita, 8.5-6, 15.6)

Illicit sex is the cornerstone of sinful life because it is the one thing that keeps us bound to this material world more than anything else. Sex is considered the highest form of material enjoyment. If we are attached to this kind of enjoyment, why would God want to remove us from it? One may ask the question, "Well, what is wrong with sex? I enjoy it. I don't see any harm in it." It is not that the Vedas prescribe one to completely give up the practice, but rather it should be regulated. One can see the negative effects of unregulated sex life in society today. Teenage pregnancy, "deadbeat dads", single parenthood, poverty, and sexually transmitted diseases are some of the more widespread problems caused by unchecked sexual activity. Instead of trying to get people to abstain from such activity, our leaders today encourage illicit sex by pushing the use of contraceptives such as condoms and birth control. No form of birth control is foolproof, so many of the unwanted pregnancies that result are then terminated through abortion, a practice which is condoned by the government. Illicit sex life is sinful as it is, but killing an innocent child in the womb is a most abominable act.

Poverty is a problem that most of today's world leaders are focused on solving. Their solutions typically focus around massive redistribution of wealth programs, but the cure for poverty actually lies elsewhere. According to statistics, in America if one graduates high school, gets married, stays married, and only has children while they are married, then they have a very low probability for living in poverty.

"...Let's examine some numbers from the Census Bureau's 2004 Current Population Survey. There's one segment of the black population that suffers only a 9.9 percent poverty rate, and only 13.7 percent of their under-5-year-olds are poor. There's another segment of the black population that suffers a 39.5 percent poverty rate, and 58.1 percent of its under-5-year-olds are poor. Among whites, one population segment suffers a 6 percent poverty rate, and only 9.9

percent of its under-5-year-olds are poor. Another segment of the white population suffers a 26.4 percent poverty rate, and 52 percent of its under-5-year-olds are poor. What do you think distinguishes the high and low poverty populations? The only statistical distinction between both the black and white populations is marriage. There is far less poverty in married-couple families..." (Walter E Williams, Are the Poor Getting Poorer?)

The Vedas advise one to get married as soon as there is any inkling of sex desire. In males especially, sex desire is very strong. We see evidence of this all around us, for people are always looking for new ways to enhance their sexual experiences. Internet pornography is a huge business, and today's television shows and movies keep getting more and more raunchy. In the traditional *varnashrama* dharma system, boys wanting to enter into family life would get married to a suitable girl as soon as they finished school, all arranged by the parents of both parties. In this way, sex life is allowed, but in a regulated manner. The husband and wife can live together peacefully, leaving time to focus on the real aim of life, service to Krishna. This type of mentality is in stark contrast to the modern day notion of men "sowing their wild oats". It is quite typical for college age men and those in their twenties to have multiple female partners, jumping from one girlfriend to the next until they find someone that suits their needs. Men and women both have more freedom today than they used to, but it has come at a cost. In the Vedic system, the husband is required to provide complete protection to the wife in all circumstances. Even those men that take to the renounced order of life, sannyasa, they make sure that the wife is taken care of by the eldest son or other family members in their absence. In today's world, men are free to exploit women, getting what they can out of them without taking any responsibility for their well-being. Such a system will always always lead to chaos.

As with all our problems, we need only look to Krishna for the solution. Bhakti yoga, or devotional service, is the highest dharma for every person in any age. The Mahabharata declares that one should avoid attachment to the four pillars of sinful life: meat eating, gambling, intoxication, and illicit sex life. One who avoids these activities while regularly chanting the maha-mantra, **"Hare Krishna Hare Krishna, Krishna Krishna, Hare Hare, Hare Rama Hare Rama, Rama Rama, Hare Hare"**, will be free from all sinful reactions. We aren't required to just give up sinful activity and sit in meditation all day. Rather we should engage in devotional service by reading about Krishna, offering Him prayers, preparing and distributing prasadam, and regularly viewing the *archa-vigraha* or deity of the Lord. The husband and wife who engage in this activity together will live very peacefully and happily. Illicit sex desire will then go away on its own.

Feeling Right At Home

"Happy shall I live there as if in my paternal house, giving no thought upon the prosperity of the three worlds, thinking only of the services that are to be rendered to my husband." (Sita Devi speaking to Lord Rama, Valmiki Ramayana, Ayodhya Kand, Sec 27)

Most of us tend to have fond memories of our childhood home. As youths, we were under the protection of our mother and father, so feelings of nostalgia arise when remembering such a time. Material life means always hankering after things we want and lamenting over things that we don't have. In Sanskrit they are referred to as *shochati* and *kankshati*:

"... The material civilization means, *shochati kankshati*, two businesses. *Kankshati* means desiring. While the body is moving we are desiring, making plans: 'I want this. I want this. My son requires this. My nation requires this. My community requires this.' This is *kankshati*; desiring to possess this, possess... And when the body is lost, then *shochati*: 'Oh, my father is lost. My brother is lost. My son is lost.' Two businesses. So as long there is no spiritual knowledge, we have got on the material conception of the body two businesses— *shochati, kankshati*: desiring for things which we do not possess and lamenting for things which we have lost." (Shrila Prabhupada, Lecture, 751017BG.JOH)

Remembering our childhood lets us escape these feelings. Eating dinner with our parents, watching television, playing in our yard; these were the primary activities of our youth that we now miss. Home is where we felt most comfortable and secure.

When we grow up to be adults, we get married and raise our families in a new home different from the one we grew up in. We hanker after independence and thus we want to start new traditions and create new memories with our spouse and children. Even so, the home of our parents, the home where we grew up and felt most comfortable, that is the home that we usually prefer.

According to Vedic philosophy, we are all individual spirit souls existing eternally as part and parcel of Lord Krishna, the Supreme Personality of Godhead. We have fallen into this material world due to our desire to lord it over and to imitate God. We mistakenly identify ourselves as the doer of activities, taking credit for the fruits of our material actions, when in fact God and His energies are responsible for everything. Trapped in the mindset of thinking in terms of "I" and "mine", we develop karma and are forced to live by its effects. We are forced to constantly transmigrate between bodies, sometimes as animals, and sometimes as human beings. Any feelings we have of so-called happiness are only temporary.

Real happiness comes from association with Krishna. When one is in the company of God, lovingly serving Him, then one becomes infused with pure bliss resulting from spiritual happiness. When Lord Rama, the incarnation of Lord Krishna in the Treta Yuga, appeared on this earth, He played the part of a young prince, the eldest son of the King of Ayodhya, Maharaja Dashratha. Due to bad judgment on the king's part, Lord Rama was ordered to spend fourteen years living as a recluse in the forest. Married to His wife Sita Devi at the time, the Lord went to inform her of the bad news and to try to convince her to not accompany Him. Sita rejected His appeal and put forth her own plea to the Lord to allow her to follow Him. Sita told Rama that living in the forest with Him would be just like living in her parents' house.

Sita Devi grew up in the royal kingdom of Maharaja Janaka and his wife Sunayana. Janaka was the highly respected king of Mithila, coming from a long line of pious kings who were also known as Janaka. Sita was his most precious jewel, someone he loved more than life itself. Being naturally pious from her birth, Sita was afforded all the regal comforts while growing up. Yet at the same time, she was not spoiled in any way, for she was trained in austerity and virtue by her parents. In Vedic culture, when a girl is married off, she in essence relinquishes all ties to her original family and adopts her husband's family as her own. Such a transition is not very easy, but Sita managed it without a problem due to her devotion to dharma and to Rama.

Sita Devi's above referenced statement describes how devotees feel when they are in God's company. The Vedas tell us that there are three worlds or planetary systems belonging to the material creation: *bhur*, *bhuva*, and *svah*.

"Heaven (*svah*) was established as the residence of the demigods, Bhuvarloka (*bhuva*) as that of the ghostly spirits, and the earth system (*bhur*) as the place of human beings and other mortal creatures. Those mystics who strive for liberation are promoted beyond these three divisions." (Lord Krishna, Shrimad Bhagavatam, 11.24.12)

Equivalent to the concept of heaven, *svah loka* is the planetary system intended for those who are pious and situated in the mode of goodness. Such people ascend to *svah loka* where they can enjoy heavenly comforts for a period of time commensurate with the weight of their good deeds. Beyond these heavenly planets are even more planets such as Satyaloka, Maharloka and Janaloka, which are reserved for those yogis seeking liberation.

"Lord Brahma created the region below the earth for the demons and the Naga snakes. In this way the destinations of the three worlds were arranged as the corresponding reactions for different kinds of work performed within the three modes of nature. By mystic yoga, great austerities and the renounced order of life, the pure destinations of Maharloka, Janaloka, Tapoloka and Satyaloka are attained. But by devotional yoga, one achieves My transcendental abode." (Lord Krishna, Shrimad Bhagavatam, 11.24.13-14)

Pure devotees don't find material comforts to be very appealing, for they prefer the direct association of Krishna. Only through devotional service can one enter the highest planets, God's personal abode, after giving up their present body.

Devotees like Sita prefer to always be with God or to always think about Him, wherever they may be. When one is in complete Krishna consciousness, then all material desires become immediately eradicated. Sita Devi was Goddess Lakshmi herself, the eternal consort of Lord Narayana, a form of Krishna. Sita is always in complete Krishna consciousness, and thus has no desire for any material rewards or enjoyments offered by the three worlds. Lord Rama was very worried that His wife would be unhappy living an austere life in the forest, a place which was meant for wild animals, beasts, and certainly not for human beings. Sita made sure to tell Him that such tough conditions wouldn't affect her because the Lord would be with her. So we should all take her lesson to heart and try to give up our hopes and dreams for material enjoyment. True bliss comes from serving God. If we always chant His name, **"Hare Krishna Hare Krishna, Krishna Krishna, Hare Hare, Hare Rama Hare Rama, Rama Rama, Hare Hare"** and follow the processes of devotional service, then we will feel at home wherever we are.

The Lord of Earth

"It is accepted that the state is the representative of God. Therefore the state's first business is to make citizens God-conscious. That is the state's first business. Any state who is neglecting this duty, he immediately becomes unqualified to hold the state office, either he may be president or the king." (Shrila Prabhupada)

A hot topic in the news a few months back was the collapse of the housing market. Five or six years ago, the government encouraged people to buy homes instead of just renting apartments. Even if people couldn't afford to buy a new house, the government offered incentives to allow them to "live the American dream." Congress forced regulated mortgage companies like Fannie Mae and Freddie Mac to lend money to people who weren't qualified to receive the loans. The motive behind the move was to increase *fairness* and provide *affordable housing*. While their intentions may have been noble, the result was a complete collapse of the banking industry due to the nonpayment of these loans.

Beginning with the last president and continuing with the new one, the government's policy is now to bail out these ailing banks by providing them money for their sustainability. As part of the process, the government is subsidizing the failed mortgages for the people who couldn't afford to pay them. A well known stock trader, Rick Santelli, lashed out at the president on cable television.

"The government is promoting bad behavior! How this, president and new administration, why didn't you put up a website to have people vote on the Internet as a referendum to see if we really want to subsidize the losers' mortgages or would we like to at least buy cars and buy houses in foreclosure and give 'em to people that might have a chance to actually prosper down the road and reward people that could carry the water instead of drink the water. This is America! How many of you people want to pay for your neighbor's mortgage that has an extra bathroom and can't pay their bills? Raise their hand. (boos) President Obama, are you listening?"

News quickly spread about Santelli's rant, and word finally reached the Obama Administration. The president's press secretary, Robert Gibbs, told reporters that the president and others were laughing at Santelli's anger and rage. Gibbs went on to say, "I think we left a few months ago the adage that if it was good for a derivatives trader, that it was good for Main Street. I think the verdict is in on that."

Herein lies the flaw with today's government and society in general. Rick Santelli and other derivatives traders are citizens just like everybody else. They have an equal right to the protections afforded by government. Most of today's leaders, including President Obama, look at society in groups. They pit classes of people against each other by favoring one group at the expense of another. The law-abiding tax payers of the country did nothing wrong, and they have a legitimate gripe when they see their tax dollars transferred to people who made bad decisions.

According to Vedic philosophy, one should not be a king, a spiritual master, or a father, unless they can release their dependents from the cycle of birth and death. A leader's job is to provide protection to all the people, and to impart spiritual knowledge on them. Protection should be provided to all the citizens equally, without favoring anyone. During Vedic times, the brahmanas were the only group that enjoyed preferential treatment. The priestly class of men were involved in pious activity, studying the Vedas, and performing sacrifices for the benefit of society as a whole. Voluntarily accepting an austere lifestyle, the kings would regularly give in charity to them, for a society requires an intelligentsia which can provide spiritual guidance. Aside from the brahmanas, a leader's role is to administer justice fairly and equally.

"Obliged we have been, since good Rama capable of reading character, will be the lord of earth, and our protector. He is of a heart devoid of arrogance, and is learned, and righteous-souled, and affectionate to his brothers. Raghava loves us even as he does his own brothers." (citizens of Ayodhya, Valmiki Ramayana, **Ayodhya Kanda, Sec 6)**

Lord Rama, an incarnation of Lord Krishna during the Treta Yuga, was set to be installed as the new king of Ayodhya by His father Maharaja Dashratha. The citizens of the town heard about this news and were greatly excited. They all loved Rama very much and they knew that He cared for everyone equally. A good leader provides protection for everyone and doesn't play favorites. Since He was God Himself, He had perfect qualifications for becoming a monarch. Lord Rama specifically incarnated to show us the proper path of dharma, and to bestow His mercy upon all the people of the world.

Not only Rama, but all the kings descending from Maharaja Ikshvaku exhibited similar behavior. A leader's duty is to create an atmosphere conducive to the cultivation of spiritual knowledge. Leaders today are themselves *karmis*, so they view *artha*, or economic development, as the primary mission in life. According to Vedic injunctions, the king, or leader of a country, is God's representative in matters of administering justice and providing protection. Whether someone owns their own home, rents, or lives with family members, they are all equally entitled to the mercy of the Lord delivered through His representatives.

Lord Rama would regularly hold town hall meetings where people could question Him directly. No one was laughed at, and all the people were treated fairly. They knew He loved all of them, and they were loyal to Him in return. Today's leaders would be well advised to learn from God's example.

Back to Basics

"One can understand the Supreme Personality as He is only by devotional service. And when one is in full consciousness of the Supreme Lord by such devotion, he can enter into the kingdom of God." (Lord Krishna, Bhagavad-gita, 18.55)

The Bhagavad-gita is one of the most famous religious books in the world. Great scholars, religionists, and devotees have studied the Gita in great detail for thousands of years. Though only a very small chapter of a much larger book, the Mahabharata, it captures the essence of Vedic philosophy.

The eternity of the soul, what happens to us when we die, what causes are happiness and distress; all these topics are covered in the Gita, which contains great quotes such as:

"As a person puts on new garments, giving up old ones, similarly, the soul accepts new material bodies, giving up the old and useless ones." (Lord Krishna, Bg 2.22)

"This individual soul is unbreakable and insoluble, and can be neither burned nor dried. He is everlasting, all-pervading, unchangeable, immovable and eternally the same." (Lord Krishna, Bg 2.24)

To most people, such knowledge is a revelation. In American schools, religion isn't taught. The Establishment Clause of the First Amendment of the Constitution declares that the Congress cannot declare an official religion for all the people of the country. This has since been misinterpreted to mean that there is a "separation of church and state" which outlaws all mention of God in the public arena. Lawyers today are on a mission to eradicate religion as much as possible from the public realm, though that wasn't the actual intention of the framers of the Constitution. Though their logic was flawed in many areas, the founding fathers were very religious people. One need only read George Washington's first Thanksgiving Proclamation in 1789 to see just how much God was on the minds of the people.

We don't hear about religion in the news unless it's a story about some priest or religious leader involved in a scandal. Due to this lack of spiritual education, most people spend their entire lives unaware of the teachings of the Bhagavad-gita.

Since it is spoken by Lord Krishna, The Supreme Personality of Godhead, the Bhagavad-gita garners the highest respect from the devotees of Krishna. Though it contains information of the highest import, such information is actually only the beginning of spiritual understanding. The Gita's most important message is that if we think of Krishna at the time of our death, then our soul will not return to this material world and it will stay with Krishna in the spiritual world forever.

"And whoever, at the time of death, quits his body, remembering Me alone, at once attains My nature. Of this there is no doubt. Whatever state of being one remembers when he quits his body, that state he will attain without fail… That abode of Mine is not illumined by the sun or moon, nor by electricity. One who reaches it never returns to this material world." (Lord Krishna, Bg, 8.5-6, 15.6)

Such information is important to know, but how do we actually achieve this goal? The Gita presents theoretical knowledge, which forms the starting point of our spiritual understanding. Theoretical knowledge is referred to as *jnana* in Sankskrit. It forms the foundation, but to actually understand what we have learned, we need practical knowledge, known as *vijnana*. For example, one may read about how to fly an airplane, taking various tests and so forth, but one doesn't truly understand what piloting involves until they actually get into the cockpit and practice flying the plane themselves. It is only then they get a real understanding of what it means to be a pilot. This same principle holds true in others areas of life. We never truly understand the difficulties our parents faced in raising us until we actually become parents ourselves.

To understand God and to know Him, we have to take to the process of devotional service. Technically known as bhakti yoga, devotional service is the process where we dovetail all our activities with Krishna, or God. If we train ourselves to always think of God during the day, learning to love Him, then surely we will think of Him at the time of death.

Hearing is one of the most important processes of devotional service. If we hear stories about Lord Krishna, then we can gradually understand who He is. We should all naturally love God simply for who He is, but the Lord is still kind enough to come to this material world from time to time and enact pastimes simply for our benefit. By reading stories about Him, we gradually develop an attachment. One can read about Lord Krishna's pastimes over and over again and never get bored.

We can find these stories in the Puranas, written by Vyasadeva. One would be hard-pressed to find any historical personality who authored more literature than Vyasadeva. He didn't write simply for entertainment's sake either, for his works are all of the highest quality since they expound the meaning of the Vedas. There are eighteen major Purnanas, and each one is quite lengthy. The Bhagavata Purana, or Shrimad-Bhagavatam, is considered the highest Purana since it covers Lord Krishna's birth and childhood pastimes in great detail.

"The Bhagavad-gita is the preliminary study of Shrimad Bhagavatam. Just like before learning any literature, one has to read the first book, ABCD. The Bhagavad-gita is the ABCD. It is just beginning of understanding of what is God. ABC. When one has passed the entrance examination, then he gets the opportunity of studying Shrimad Bhagavatam." (Shrila Prabhupada, 730227rc.jkt)

After reading Bhagavad-gita, we should all make an effort to read the Bhagavatam and take the next step in rekindling our love for Krishna. Due to our imperfect senses, we can never truly understand God, but by reading stories about Him, as told by His great devotees, we will gradually understand Him better. By knowing and loving God, we automatically book our return flight home, back to Godhead.

Sanatana Dharma

"I shall sport with you, Oh great hero, in that forest impregnated with the fragrance of flowers, tending you constantly, having my senses subdued, and being engaged in austere performances." (Sita Devi speaking to Lord Rama, Valmiki Ramayana, Ayodhya Kand, Sec 27)

In loving relationships, we often subordinate ourselves to the wishes of our paramour. Those who are in love will often utter the phrase "I will dedicate my life to making you happy" to their significant other. Such sentiment is very nice because it represents the essence of true love. Wanting more for the other person than you want for yourself is the quintessential ingredient of love.

A husband or wife will often put themselves into very stressful situations in order that they may please their spouse. Sometimes a husband will go to great lengths to buy his wife some nice jewelry or some flowers to mark a special occasion such as an anniversary or birthday. A loving wife will similarly go through the pains of cooking elaborate meals, or attending sporting events, or travelling to exotic destinations simply to give pleasure to her husband. Many times we don't like performing these tasks but if it makes our spouse happy then we are more than willing to do it. For we know if our husband or wife is happy and satisfied, then we are happy.

Lord Rama, who was God Himself living in Ayodhya many thousands of years ago, was given the order by His father, King Dashratha, to live in the forest as a recluse for fourteen years. Being married at the time to His wife Sita, the Lord knew that she would insist on coming along. Rama gave her many sound reasons why she should remain in the kingdom under the protection of other family members, but Sita soundly rejected them. Being truly in love with Lord Rama, Sita would not be happy unless her Lord was happy. Lord Rama was very worried about how Sita would fare in the forest, since the conditions would be very rough and not suitable for a woman accustomed to a life of royalty. To alleviate Rama's worries, Sita assured Him that she would constantly tend to Him and that she would be engaged in austerities.

Aside from exhibiting her love for Rama, Sita Devi in this instance is teaching all of us the proper way to serve God. We all want to serve something in this material world, whether it is our senses, our bosses, our parents, our children, or even our lovers. While all those types of service may be very nice, our original occupation is to serve Krishna, or God. According to Vedic philosophy, this is called *sanatana dharma*. *Sanatana* means that which has no begging or end and *dharma* means occupation. Sometimes dharma is mistakenly interpreted to mean religion, but religion has a different connotation. One's religious belief system may change from Hindu to Muslim or Christian to Jew, but one's occupational duty never changes. That is the true definition of dharma.

"Religion conveys the idea of faith. Faith may change. One may have faith in a particular process, and he may change the faith afterwards and adopt another faith. But sanatana-dharma means which cannot be changed. Just like water and liquidity. Liquidity cannot be changed from water. Heat and fire. Heat cannot be changed from fire. Similarly, the eternal function of the eternal living entity, which is known as sanatana-dharma, cannot be changed. It is not possible to change. We have to find out what is that eternal function of the eternal living entity. When we speak of sanatana-dharma therefore, we must take it for granted on the authority of Shripada Ramanujacharya that it has no beginning nor any end." (Shrila Prabhupada, Lecture)

Sanatana dharma means our eternal occupation. It is our duty to serve the Lord since that is what we are naturally inclined to do. In order to serve the Lord, we must voluntarily submit ourselves to austerity or pennance, which is known as *tapasya*.

Sita Devi informed Lord Rama that she was more than willing to perform *tapasya* for Him in the forest. "I will always serve you with all my heart and soul. I will undergo and any all hardships simply to make you happy. You are my Lord for life, and what may be viewed as hardships to others, will be undertaken by me with glee and enthusiasm. Fear not for my welfare in the forest. If I am serving you, then I will always be happy, and thus you will be too." These were the thoughts she was conveying to Lord Rama. This is the attitude of a pure devotee who is most highly advanced. By following the principles of devotional service through chanting the Lord's names, offering Him prayers, rendering service to His deity, and by voluntarily abstaining from the primary sinful activities of life, namely meat eating, gambling, intoxication, and illicit sex, then God will be most pleased with us, and we in turn can enjoy an eternal blissful relationship with Him.

Animal Sacrifice

"The humble sage, by virtue of true knowledge, sees with equal vision a learned and gentle brahmana, a cow, an elephant, a dog and a dog-eater." (Lord Krishna, Bhagavad-gita, 5.18)

One of the four regulative principles of devotional service requires one to refrain from eating meat, fish, or eggs. Meat eating involves unnecessary violence towards animals, so anyone who stays away from such food will avoid the negative karma associated with it. Living a simple, non-violent lifestyle allows us to concentrate our time and energy on God realization.

One will find, however, that the concept of animal sacrifice is very prominent in the scriptures of all major religions. The Christian Bible has a detailed list of which animals can be sacrificed and how they are to be offered. Similarly, the Vedic literature lists many such animal sacrifices which reward the performer with material benedictions. During Lord Krishna's time on earth, the great king Yudhishthira performed the sacred Ashwamedha sacrifice, which involves sacrificing a horse. Prior to that, during the Treta Yuga, the famous Maharaja Dashratha of Ayodhya also performed the sacrifice. It was performed by many kings with the idea of bestowing good karma on the king and his kingdom. Dashratha's sacrifice bore fruit in the form of Lord Rama, God Himself, being born as his first son.

The performance of such sacrifices seems to contradict the principle of no meat eating. However, this type of animal sacrifice bears no resemblance to the violence committed against animals in modern day slaughterhouses. The Vedas are somewhat complex, with different dharmas (religious duty) assigned to different classes of people. Since the material world is a place governed by *gunas*, or qualities (goodness, passion, and ignorance), every living entity has a different level of intelligence and thereby varying capacities for understanding scriptural injunctions. Though *bhagavata-dharma*, loving service to God, is the highest form of religion, God is so kind that He provides other forms of religion so as to allow everyone to make spiritual advancement. Below the system of *bhagavata-dharma* is the religious system involving the four rewards of life. Those who are religiously inclined generally seek the rewards of dharma (religiosity), artha (economic development), kama (sense gratification), and moksha (liberation). To achieve these benedictions, there is a section of the Vedas known as *karma-kanda*. It is in this portion of the Vedas where one will find the various animal sacrifices performed by kings of the past. The idea wasn't to allow meat eating for simple sense gratification, but rather to sanction violence in a regulated manner, which would be both beneficial to the performer and to the animal sacrificed. In a sacrifice properly performed by qualified brahmanas wherein mantras were perfectly recited, the living entity inside the animal would immediately be rewarded a higher birth in the next life. The performer would also immediately receive the material rewards they were seeking after. Naturally, such a religious system is subordinate to *bhagavata-dharma*, but it was nonetheless performed as a way of allowing kings to make gradual elevation in spiritual consciousness. The kshatriyas, or warrior class of men, generally live in the mode of passion, *rajo-guna*. Due to this fact, they are allowed to gamble and even hunt deer as a way of practicing their defensive skills. Unnecessary violence towards animals was never condoned, and there are many historical incidents mentioned in the Vedic texts of kings being punished for acts of unnecessary violence towards deer or other living entities in the forest. The same Maharaja Dashratha once accidentally shot and killed a young boy with his arrow while ranging the forest. Since the boy's parents would eventually die from the grief resulting from the untimely separation from their son, they cursed Dashratha to suffer the same fate in the future. For this reason, Dashratha died after the exile of His eldest and most beloved son Rama.

"In the Vedic literature there are numerous prescription of sacrifice. And in some of the sacrifices animal sacrifice is also recommended. So that animal sacrifice does not mean to kill the animal. Animal sacrifice means to prove the strength of Vedic hymns so that one old animal is put into the fire and he's given again a new life, renewed life, just to show the potency of the hymns, Vedic hymns. But in this age, Kali-yuga, those sacrifices are forbidden." (Shrila Prabhupada, Lecture, 700416LE.LA)

These sacrifices were a means of testing the brahmanas who would preside over them, and was also a way of benefitting the animal being sacrificed. The entire purpose was aimed at providing purification. These sacrifices were performed during previous Yugas, where dharma had a stronger presence in society. According to the Vedas, dharma gradually declines amongst the population as time goes on. The current age we are in, Kali Yuga, is best known for dharma having only a twenty-five percent level of strength, whereas it was at one hundred percent at the beginning of creation. Gradually with this decline in religiosity, came the tainting of these sacrifices. Brahmanas were no longer performing them for purification, but merely as an excuse to eat animal flesh.

"When there was too much animal sacrifice in India, Lord Buddha appeared. And in the Vedas there is recommendation for animal sacrifice in some sacrificial ceremony, not ordinarily. And that sacrifice is meant for testing the power of chanting mantra. An animal would be put into the fire, and it would come again with renewed life. In this way, there is recommendation in the Vedas that some animals... But people misunderstood it. People began to slaughter." (Shrila Prabhupada, Room Conversation, Tokyo, 720422)

Krishna advented as Lord Buddha specifically to stop the degraded process of animal slaughter. In order to justify his message of nonviolence, he preached against the injunctions of the Vedas. In this way, the modern day injunction against meat eating was instituted and the animal sacrifice process was gradually stopped.

Meat eating involves killing another animal, which shouldn't be done. But God is so nice that He understands that many people won't be able to give up such a practice easily. Bestowing His mercy upon them, He provided for the rituals of animal sacrifice to allow them to gradually rise up the chain of God consciousness. If one sacrifices an animal before the Goddess Kali, he is at least thinking about God prior to committing such a heinous act. One will find that dishes containing goat meat are very prevalent in Indian restaurants and it stems from the tradition of sacrifice to Goddess Kali. Even a sanctioned sacrifice like that has many stringent rules attached to it. The animal must be a goat and the sacrifice can only be performed once a month. In this way, God is helping people by making meat eating such an arduous task.

"Even though one may be religiously inclined, animal sacrifice is recommended in the shashtras, not only in the Vedas but even in the modern scriptures of other sects...When such people kill animals, they can at least do so in the name of religion. However, when the religious system is transcendental, like the Vaishnava religion, there is no place for animal sacrifice." (Shrila Prabhupada, Shrimad Bhagavatam, 4.26.1-3 Purport)

The word "Vaishnava" refers to devotees of Lord Vishnu, who is the same as Lord Krishna. By following the principles of devotional service, we have no need for mundane material sacrifices. We should all try and rise to such a platform. Giving up meat eating may seem very difficult, but if we dedicate ourselves to constantly chanting the names of God in a loving way, **"Hare Krishna Hare Krishna, Krishna Krishna, Hare Hare, Hare Rama Hare Rama, Rama Rama, Hare Hare"**, then we will surely succeed.

Maintainer of the Universe

57

"Oh great hero, capable are you to maintain many thousand others in the forest, what to speak of me." (Sita Devi speaking to Lord Rama, Valmiki Ramayana, Ayodhya Kand, Sec 27)

Lord Krishna, the Supreme Personality of Godhead, maintains all the universes with their millions of planets all through His various expansions. We all know that God is great, but the Vedas describe just how great He is.

In this material world we see that men have great difficulty in maintaining even one wife. Many times they are unable to hold on to their relationship and they give way to separation and divorce. As evidenced in the Shrimad Bhagavatam, Lord Krishna was able to simultaneously maintain and please 16,108 wives during His time on earth some five thousand years ago. Narada Muni, the venerable saint of the three worlds, once came to visit Krishna in one of His palaces to see how He was faring with His primary wife Rukmini. Upon seeing the Lord happily engaged in day to day activities, Narada then went on to visit other palaces of the Lord. He was astonished to find Krishna in each and every one of them simultaneously engaged in various activities.

"In one palace Lord Krishna was found engaged in feeding brahmanas after performing ritualistic yajnas. In another palace, Narada found Krishna engaged in silently chanting the Gayatri mantra, and in a third he found Him practicing fighting with a sword and shield. In some palaces Lord Krishna was found riding on horses or elephants or chariots and wandering hither and thither. Elsewhere He was found lying down on His bedstead taking rest, and somewhere else He was found sitting in His chair, being praised by the prayers of His different devotees. In some of the palaces He was found consulting with ministers like Uddhava and others on important matters of business. In one palace He was found surrounded by many young society girls, enjoying in a swimming pool. In another palace He was found engaged in giving well-decorated cows in charity to the brahmanas, and in another palace He was found hearing the narrations of the Puranas or histories, such as the Mahabharata, which are supplementary literatures for disseminating Vedic knowledge to common people by narrating important instances in the history of the universe. Somewhere Lord Krishna was found enjoying the company of a particular wife by exchanging joking words with her. Somewhere else He was found engaged along with His wife in religious ritualistic functions. Since it is necessary for householders to increase their financial assets for various expenditures, Krishna was found somewhere engaged in matters of economic development. Somewhere else He was found enjoying family life according to the regulative principles of the shastras...Thus Narada saw one single Krishna living in sixteen thousand palaces by His plenary expansions. Due to His inconceivable energy, He was visible in each and every individual queen's palace. Lord Krishna has unlimited power, and Narada's astonishment was boundless upon observing again and again the demonstration of Lord Krishna's internal energy. Lord Krishna behaved by His personal example as if He were very much attached to the four principles of civilized life, namely religiousness, economic development, sense gratification and salvation. These four principles of material existence are necessary for the spiritual advancement of human society, and although Lord Krishna had no need to do so, He exhibited His household activities so that people might follow in His footsteps for their own interest. Lord Krishna satisfied the sage Narada in every way. Narada was very much pleased by seeing the Lord's activities in Dvaraka, and thus he departed." (Shrila Prabhupada, Krishna, The Supreme Personality of Godhead, Volume 2, Ch 2.14)

These facts seem outrageous to most non-devotees. The internet is full of discussions on the topic of Krishna and His wives. "How could Krishna have so many wives? That doesn't make sense. It must be part of the mythology." These are some of the common sentiments. However, the Vedas and the Puranas are historical records of actual events that have taken place on this planet and on other planets throughout the universe. Sometimes they even describe events that have yet to occur. Through our material senses, we may think that maintaining that many wives is impossible, but to devotees of the Lord, such a feat doesn't nearly begin to describe God's power. Krishna effortlessly created a monstrous astral body that provides heat and light to millions of species throughout the universe. This body is known as the sun and scientists have yet to begin understanding its nature. Unable to explain the phenomenon, scientists theorize that a random collision of atomic particles created the sun and the rest of creation. If such an event did occur, why are these same scientists unable to reproduce this miracle? If they harnessed all the electric power in the world and used it to turn on millions upon millions of lights, it still wouldn't come close to the power generated by the sun. We know from the Vedas that Krishna created the sun, and if God is able to create something so amazing, then maintaining many wives, or lifting a giant hill are merely child's play for Him.

When Krishna incarnated as the most pious prince of Ayodhya, Lord Rama, He willingly accepted banishment to the forest for fourteen years by His father, King Dashrata. The Lord was married to His wife Sita at the time, so He tried His best to dissuade her from following Him. Sita Devi was the Goddess of Fortune, Lakshmi, so she was completely devoted to Rama. She put forth her own set of arguments in favor of her accompanying the Lord to the forest.

According to Vedic culture, a woman is to be provided protection at all stages of her life, and not ever to be given outright independence. As a child, a girl is given protection by her father, as an adult by her husband, and in old age by the eldest son. This was the traditional system and both Lord Rama and Sita Devi were abiding by it. The

Lord wanted His wife to remain in the kingdom where she would be protected from the dangers of forest life. God is always kind to His devotees and never wants to see them in any sort of pain. Forest life is meant for the animals and for those in the renounced order of life, *sannyasis*. However, Sita Devi made it a point to remind Lord Rama that He indeed can provide protection to a limitless amount of people. She was basically saying, "You are God Himself. This entire universe is maintained by You. Millions upon millions of planets are floating in the air through Your energies. Taking care of me in the forest should be no problem for You." Due to these and other arguments put forth by Sita, the Lord was unable to stop her from coming with Him. This illustrates the power of devotional service. God loves His devotees more than His devotees love Him. For those truly surrendered souls, the Lord willingly subordinates Himself to their wishes.

Krishna Janmashtami 2009

"In order to deliver the pious and to annihilate the miscreants, as well as to reestablish the principles of religion, I advent Myself millennium after millennium." (Lord Krishna, Bhagavad-gita 4.8)

Janmashtami is the appearance day celebration of Lord Shri Krishna, the Supreme Personality of Godhead according to the Vedas, the ultimate authority on all matters of religion and life. The Lord came to this earth around five thousand years ago, towards the end of the Dvapara Yuga, in Mathura, India. Born as the eighth son of Mother Devaki, the Lord specially came to deliver His devotees. Technically, the Lord doesn't take birth since He is eternal. Therefore, the birthday of Krishna is referred to as His appearance day.

"My dear Lord, it is not a very wonderful thing that You appear within the womb of Devaki because the creation was also made in that way. You were lying in the Causal Ocean as Maha-Vishnu, and by Your breathing process, innumerable universes came into existence." (Vasudeva speaking to Krishna, Krishna, The Supreme Personality of Godhead, Volume 1, Ch 1.3)

The Lord's appearance day is celebrated by the devotees since they love to always think of the Lord and remember His pastimes. Similar to the way we celebrate birthdays, anniversaries, and other holidays, devotees celebrate the anniversary dates of occasions related to God. In the Bhagavad-gita, Lord Krishna declares that He comes to earth from time to time to reinstitute the principles of dharma and to give protection to His dependents.

During the time of Krishna's advent, there was a king named Kamsa who had amassed a great empire. Everyone lived in fear of Him due to His strength. A person of a demoniac nature, Kamsa had imprisoned his sister Devaki and her husband Vasudeva due to a prophecy that stated that Kamsa would killed by the eighth son of Devaki. As Devaki gave birth to her children, one by one Kamsa would mercilessly kill them by throwing them against a stone wall. In this way, he anxiously awaited the birth of Devaki's eighth son. Krishna, seeing this predicament, decided to appear in the womb of Devaki to fulfill the prophecy and to free Devaki and Vasudeva. After being offered prayers from the demigods, Devaki gave birth to Krishna, who then appeared in His four-handed form of Narayana, or Vishnu.

"Thus eulogized by the gods, Devaki bore in her womb the lotus-eyed Lord Krishna, the protector of the world. On the day of His birth, the quarters of the horizon were filled with joy, as if moonlight was diffused over the whole earth. The pious experienced new delight, the strong winds were hushed, and the rivers glided tranquilly when Krishna was about to be born. The seas with their own melodious murmurings provided the music, while the Kinnaras and Gandharvas danced and sang and the demigods showered down flowers upon the earth. At midnight, when the supporter of all was about to be born, the clouds emitted low pleasing sounds and poured down a rain of flowers.

As soon as Vasudeva beheld the child of the complexion of lotus leaves, having four arms, and the shrivatsa mark on His chest, he addressed Him with love and reverence saying, 'I understand that You have appeared to kill the uncivilized Kamsa and his followers. But knowing that You were to appear to kill him and his followers, he has already killed so many of Your predecessors, elder brothers. Now he is simply awaiting the news of Your birth. As soon as he hears about it, he will immediately appear with all kinds of weapons to kill You.' Devaki also exclaimed, 'My only cause of fear from my brother Kamsa is due to Your appearance. My Lord Madhusudana (Krishna), Kamsa may know that You are already born. Therefore I request You to conceal this four-armed form of Your Lordship which holds the four symbols of Vishnu. My dear Lord, at the end of the annihilation of the cosmic manifestation, You put the whole universe within Your abdomen; still by Your unalloyed mercy You have appeared in my womb. I am surprised that You imitate the activities of ordinary human beings just to please Your devotee.'

To these pleas Krishna answered and said, 'Dear mother, in former times I was prayed to by you and adored in the hope of progeny: your prayers have been granted, for I am born as your son. I know you are very concerned about Me and afraid of Kamsa. Therefore I order you to take Me immediately to Gokula and replace Me with the daughter who has just been born to Yashoda.' So saying, Vasudeva, taking the baby, went out that same night; for the guards were all charmed by Yogamaya, as were the warders at the gates of Mathura, and thus they didn't obstruct Vasudeva's path. To protect the infant from the heavy rain that fell from the clouds of night, Ananta Sesha Naga, the supporter of the universe, the serpent with unlimited hoods, followed Vasudeva and spread his hoods above their heads; and when Vasudeva, with the baby Krishna in his arms, crossed the Yamuna river, deep as it was, and dangerous with numerous whirlpools, the waters became stilled and cleared a path for Vasudeva. On the bank he saw Nanda and the rest who had come there to bring taxes due to Kamsa. At the same time Yashoda was also under the influence of Yogamaya, whom she had brought forth as her daughter, and whom the prudent Vasudeva took up, placing Krishna in her place by the side of Yashoda. He then quickly returned home. When Yashoda awaoke, she found that she had delivered a boy, as black as the dark leaves of the lotus, and she greatly rejoiced." (Story of Krishna's birth found in the Vishnu and Bhagavata Puranas)

Vyasa Puja 2009

"The Supreme Personality of Godhead is pleased to guide a devotee from within and without. From within He guides him as the Supersoul, and from without He guides him as the spiritual master." (Shrila Prabhupada, Chaitanya Charitamrita, Adi 8.79 Purport)

Vyasa Puja is the celebration of the appearance day of the spiritual master. Vyasadeva, also known as Krishna-Dwaipayana Vyasa, is the literary incarnation of Lord Krishna. He is the author of almost every significant Vedic text, which includes the four Vedas, the Puranas, the Upanishads, and the Vedanta-sutra. One will be hard-pressed to find anyone who has authored more literature in their lifetime than Vyasadeva has. The bona fide guru, or spiritual master, is one who represents Vyasadeva and his teachings.

His Divine Grace A.C. Bhaktivedanta Swami Prabhupada was the founder of the International Society for Krishna Consciousness (ISKCON), which is more commonly known as the Hare Krishna Movement. A bona fide spiritual master in the line descending from Vyasadeva, and notably Lord Chaitanya, he spread Krishna *prema*, love for God, throughout the world in a very short period of time starting in the late 1960s.

There has been a long held belief amongst many in India that the Vedas and their teachings are the sole property of Hindus, or more specifically, those born into the varnashrama dharma system. The Vedas prescribe society to be divided into four *varnas*, or classes, and one's duration of life to be divided into four *ashramas*, or modes of life. The four *varnas* are brahmana, kshatriya, vaishya, and shudra. According to the strict Vedic definition, everyone is born a shudra, meaning one who is untrained in any religious principles. This naturally makes sense since we are all born ignorant. One may be the son of a brahmana, kshatriya, or vaishya, but that doesn't automatically mean they belong to the same caste or *varna* as their father. Rather, one has to be trained by a guru and given the sacred thread, which signifies the second and more important birth. However, over time the system in India degraded to a point where people started claiming to belong to a certain caste simply by birth. Investiture of the sacred thread was done more as a formality, for no one was taking any training from a guru. This practice is still going on, with many claiming to be brahmanas (priestly class) simply by birthright, though they engage in all sorts of sinful activity such as meat eating, gambling, and intoxication.

Those claiming brahminical status simply from birthright do so because they have some lineage to a famous rishi of the past, such as Kashyapa, Vashishta, Katyanana, Upamanyu, etc. These were all great brahmanas of the past, and one will find stories about them in the Purnanas, Ramayana, and other Vedic texts. While it is certainly very nice to have a family lineage that goes back that far, simply being born in a high family isn't enough. One has to exhibit the qualities and work, guna and karma, to be classified as part of a certain caste.

"According to the three modes of material nature and the work ascribed to them, the four divisions of human society were created by Me. And, although I am the creator of this system, you should know that I am yet the non-doer, being unchangeable." (Lord Krishna, Bhagavad-gita, 4.13)

Lord Krishna declares that one's caste should be determined by qualities (*guna*) that are inherent in them and by the work (karma) that they perform. In this manner, varnashrama dharma is actually open to anyone, provided they are trained by a bona fide spiritual master. Lord Chaitanya Mahaprabhu, Krishna Himself, was the first person to really spread Krishna *prema* to those born outside of the Hindu religion. This is the character of a true saint, for he believes that Krishna's mercy should be made available to anyone and everyone, regardless of what family they were born into. By teaching others about Krishna, and urging them to become His devotees, one performs the highest service to his fellow man.

In 1965, A. C. Bhaktivedanta Swami Prabhupada brought Lord Chaitanya's movement to America. His own spiritual master, Shrila Bhaktisiddhanta Sarasvati Goswami Prabhupada, urged Shrila Prabhupada to translate the great Vedic texts into English and spread the message to the Western world. Shrila Prabhupada took this directive very seriously and his sincere efforts spawned a worldwide movement which continues to this very day. Krishna is now a household name known throughout the world.

Those born into Hindu families are very fortunate in that they know about Krishna from their very childhood. Almost every Hindu family has some sort of altar in their home, whereby they regularly perform *arati* at least twice a day. Though they might not offer everything they eat to the Lord, they make sure to offer Him some type of sweet at least twice a day, distributing the prasadam to their friends and family. Being a part of such family traditions, one naturally grows up to have a deep love and respect for Lord Krishna, Lord Rama, Sita, Ganesha, and especially Hanuman. The stories of the Ramayana and Mahabharata are known to almost all Hindus, for in India there are many books and movies about them.

But what about those who aren't born into such a family? Where does that leave them? Thanks to Shrila Prabhupada, millions of people around the world became acquainted with Vedic culture. He turned thousands of whites, blacks, men, women, Americans, Europeans, and others, whether they were Indian or not, into perfect brahmanas by requiring them to strictly adhere to the four regulative principles (no meat eating, gambling, intoxication, and illicit sex) and to regularly chant the maha-mantra: "Hare Krishna Hare Krishna, Krishna

Krishna, Hare Hare, Hare Rama Hare Rama, Rama Rama, Hare Hare." Considering how engrained meat eating and intoxication are in the Western culture, such a feat was nothing short of a miracle.

Though no longer physically present in this world, Prabhupada continues to teach to this day through His many books and recorded lectures. On this occasion of Vyasa Puja, let us humbly offer our obeissances to a true *jagad-guru*. Shrila Prabhupada ki jai!.

Fasting

71

"Work done as a sacrifice for Vishnu has to be performed, otherwise work binds one to this material world. Therefore, O son of Kunti, perform your prescribed duties for His satisfaction, and in that way you will always remain unattached and free from bondage." (Lord Krishna, Bhagavad-gita, 3.9)

Lent is the holy period in the Catholic calendar where someone gives up something, a form of sense gratification which is usually meat eating, voluntarily. The Lent period lasts for forty days, so those accustomed to regularly eating meat scramble to find ways to adhere to the fast.

Lent is generally viewed unfavorably by the younger generation. "Why is God punishing us? Why can't we just eat what we want?" These are some of the questions posed by followers of the faith. In actuality, most people don't even adhere to the regulations of Lent. Those who are aware of it, often look for loopholes and excuses to continue their meat eating. "Oh fish doesn't count. I can eat that. I can most certainly eat eggs. What about chicken? That's not really meat right?" The Catholic Church had a long-standing rule stating that people couldn't eat meat on Fridays. That rule has since been abolished due to the fact that no one was following it.

The concept of fasting is present in all major religions. The Muslims have the Ramadan Holiday where one is prohibited from taking food during daylight hours. The Vedas, the ancient scriptures of India, probably have the most comprehensive list of fasting regulations. Those of us who grew up in Hindu families are very familiar with many of them. Our parents and elder relatives were always abiding by some type of fast. "Oh today is Tuesday. I don't eat on Tuesday...I can't eat anything with salt in it today...I can only eat fruits and drink water today." These were some of the statements we commonly heard as children growing up. It seemed very puzzling to us, since we generally just ate whatever we wanted whenever we wanted. What was the point of starving yourself? Many Hindu women even fast for Teej, which is an annual holiday dedicated to ensuring a long life for husbands.

Fasting is rooted in the concept of *tapasya*. Tapasya means austerities or the voluntary acceptance of penance. This isn't any ordinary type of penance either. Tapasya is meant specifically to be for spiritual advancement, a completely religious activity. Tapasya works because it involves serving the Lord. As living entities, our natural instinct is to serve ourselves. Not necessarily selfishness, but acting in our own self-interest. The entire free-market capitalist system is built around this notion. People acting in their own self-interest, which leads to an overall favorable condition economically. The Vedas, however, tell us that this life is meant for serving Krishna, or God, and not our senses. It is for this reason that tapasya was introduced. Breaking free of the bodily concept of life is very difficult. Everyone is identifying with their gross material body, something which they are forced to give up at the time of death. I may be an Indian in this life, but in my next life, I can very well be born as an American or a Muslim. Knowing that fact, our nationality, skin color, or ethnicity isn't important. At our core, we are spirit souls, *aham brahmasmi*. As spirit souls part and parcel of God, our business as human beings is to reconnect with Him. That is the ultimate aim of life. In order to truly realize this fact, we have to break free from our attachment to sense gratification. Austerities help us do that.

There is a common expression that says "What doesn't kill you makes you stronger." Though not true in all circumstances, with respect to tapasya, it is generally the case. By periodically abstaining from certain kinds of food, or all food in general, we actually become stronger because our minds become clearer. Many of us spend some time during the day thinking about what to eat for lunch or dinner. "Oh where should I go for lunch? I just went to such and such a place yesterday.

I feel like something different today." Even if we are eating food that we like, we tend to get sick of eating the same thing over and over again. We're always looking for ways to satisfy our taste buds. Thinking about food may seem harmless, but that time could be better spent thinking about God. This is where tapasya comes. If we spent the day fasting, we most certainly would think about our hunger during the day. Now ordinarily, this wouldn't be a good thing, since we would be unnecessarily causing ourselves stress. However, if we fast for God, then anytime we think of our hunger during the day, we immediately will think of Him. That is always a good thing. Sometimes men will get into fights or brawls and receive bruises and other wounds as a result. Most men love to show off these wounds to others, because it is a symbol of their toughness and what they went through. In a similar fashion, the hunger pains as a result of fasting for Krishna is a sort of war wound, something we receive as a result of our dedication to the Lord. It is something we can be proud of.

The major occasions for fasting coincide with the appearance day anniversaries of the Lord and His associates. Krishna Janmashtami is generally considered the most important day of the year for followers of the Vedic tradition since it marks the appearance day anniversary of Lord Krishna. Since Mother Devaki gave birth to Krishna at midnight, devotees usually observe a complete fast on Janmashtami leading up until midnight. People fast for the occasions of Rama Navami and Radhashtami in a similar manner. There are so many specific fasts prescribed in the Vedas for different purposes, but the two most widely observed regular fasts are Ekadashi and Purnima. The entire Vedic calendar revolves around the lunar cycle, so Ekadashi and Purnima are specific days in that cycle. Purnima represents the full moon day, and followers of the Satyanarayana Vrata fast specifically on these days. Devotees perform Katha of Lord Shri Satyanarayana, and then eat the prasadam that is offered to Him. Ekadashi is another specific day in the lunar cycle, an occasion observed specifically by Vaishnavas, or devotees of Vishnu. In a strict sense, devotees are supposed to observe a completely fast on this day, but the regulation has been loosened a bit. Generally, devotees simply abstain from eating grains (rice, bread, etc.) and beans on this day.

Vedic literature is full of people performing tapasya and receiving a benefit as a result. Mother Parvati performed severe austerities in the forest for many years and was rewarded by getting Lord Shiva for a husband. Lord Rama and Sita observed a fast the night before the initial date set for the Lord's installation as successor to His father, the king of Ayodhya. In this way, God and other great personalities set a good example for the rest of us to follow. If one can fast without inflicting too much pain on oneself, then it is definitely worth trying. Tapasya is one of the most important tools in a transcendentalist's arsenal. It can help us break free of the repeated cycle of birth and death, and bring us back home after this life, back to Godhead.

Not To Be Denied

"Surely shall I go today to the forest with you; there is no doubt about it and you shall not be able, Oh great hero, to dissuade me from so doing." (Sita Devi speaking to Lord Rama, Valmiki Ramayana, Ayodhya Kand, Sec 27)

Sometimes when we take up a new task, we have difficulty in finishing it. We may decide to take up the process of learning to play guitar only to have the guitar sitting underneath our bed after attempting to play it only a few times. We may decide to start keeping a journal that we intend write in nightly, only to find that that the journal is left by itself in a drawer after only a few entries.

We seem to come up with new projects that we are never able to finish. What gets in the way? According to Vedic philosophy, this material world has an all-pervading illusory energy called *maya* that is the root cause of most of our problems. It is due to maya's influence that we falsely identify with our gross material body and thus constantly seek pleasure in mundane sense gratification. Completing new tasks becomes difficult because maya is always pulling our attention elsewhere telling us that we will be more happy doing something else.

Taking up the process of devotional service is just as difficult as taking up new hobbies. Most people that we know are immersed in material life and have no interest whatsoever in spiritual matters. Lord Krishna Himself declares in the Bhagavad-gita that it is only after millions of births that one finally comes to a proper understanding of their constitutional position as spirit soul part and parcel of God:

"After many births and deaths, he who is actually in knowledge surrenders unto Me, knowing Me to be the cause of all causes and all that is. Such a great soul is very rare." (Bg 7.19)

Taking up spiritual life means one has to declare war on maya. Maya doesn't give up so easily, so she puts even more impediments in our way.

"When we accept any self-realization process, it is practically declaring war against the illusory energy, maya. So when there's a question of maya or a question of fight or war there will be so many difficulties imposed by maya; that is certain. Therefore there is a chance of failure, but one has to become very steady." (Shrila Prabhupada, Lecture, Los Angeles, Feb 20, 1969)

Our friends and family start to question what we are doing. "Why are you chanting? Who is this Krishna that you always talk about? You must be so lost to have gotten into all this mysticism." These are the phrases commonly uttered by those who aren't familiar with the processes of devotional service.

Now these people can't really be blamed for their ignorance. We can get so bound up in material life that something so natural as chanting God's name can seem foreign to us. Just as with playing guitar or training for marathons, for one to be successful in in devotional life they have to have steadiness of mind and perseverance.

"...one must take up a particular path and stick to it, obeying all the rules and regulations necessary for success in spiritual life." (Shril Prabhupada, Chaitanya Charitamrita Introduction)

Lord Rama, who was God Himself playing the role of a human being on earth, was ordered to spend fourteen years in the forest by His father King Dashratha of Ayodhya. Rama's wife Sita desperately wanted to accompany the Lord during the exile period, so she put forth a series of arguments in hopes of persuading the Lord. After reiterating the proper duties of a wife, Sita finally declared that there was no way for the Lord to stop her from coming along. Such determination illustrates just how pure a devotee Sita was.

Having grown up in the royal court of King Janaka of Mithila, Sita was accustomed to having all the material comforts of life. Even nowadays, common folk are so enamored by royal life that they follow all the goings on of the queen of England and her children. Members of the press dream of a life of advanced material sense gratification, so they try to live vicariously through those who already enjoy the high life. Even faced with every material distraction, Sita Devi was so steady of mind that she was completely devoted to God, who happened to be her husband. Lord Rama knew just how devoted she was, so He was forced to acquiesce and allow her to accompany Him. Devotional life begins by following the rules and regulations given to us by our spiritual master, namely voluntarily performing austerities with the goal of gaining spiritual understanding. From Sita Devi's example, we see that by sticking to these regulations, we can confidently declare victory over maya. God rewards our victory by allowing us to always be in His company.

Material life means we are a slave to our senses. By constantly chanting the Lord's holy name, "Hare Krishna Hare Krishna, Krishna Krishna, Hare Hare, Hare Rama Hare Rama, Rama Rama, Hare Hare", the tables get turned, and the slave becomes the master. The title of Goswami actually means "master of the senses". One who is directly engaged in God's service, giving up all hopes and dreams of sense gratification, surrendering everything unto to Him, that person is a Goswami. Though a tender and delicate woman, Sita was actually the greatest of transcendentalists, firm and steady in her vow of devotion. Therefore she is worthy of our highest love and respect.

God is One

"Since everyone has a different body and mind, different types of religions are needed. But when one is situated on the spiritual platform, there are no bodily and mental differences. Consequently on the absolute platform there is oneness in religion." (Shrila Prabhupada, Chaitanya Charitamrita, Madhya 17.184 Purport)

Jesus, Allah, Buddha, Krishna...God has many different names according to different religions. People may ask one another, "Who is your God? Who do you worship?" Though God may have many different names, He is still one. There isn't a separate God for Hindus and a separate God for Christians or those following other faiths.

Seeing all the different religions that have existed since the beginning of time, one may think that God is just a man-made creation. This is a common sentiment amongst atheists and pseudo-intellectuals. Though it might seem plausible, the actual fact is that God appears in different forms based on time and circumstance. According to Vedic philosophy, God appears personally on earth when there is a general decline in dharma, or religiosity, amongst the people.

"Whenever and wherever there is a decline in religious practice, O descendant of Bharata, and a predominant rise of irreligion-at that time I descend Myself." (Lord Krishna, Bhagavad-gita, 4.7)

Lord Krishna, the Supreme Personality of Godhead, has incarnated throughout history in different forms such as Lord Narasimha, Lord Rama, and even personally as Himself. His specific purpose was different each time. Lord Narasimha came to kill the evil demon Hiranyakashipu, who was tormenting his devotee son, Prahlada. Lord Rama came to kill the demon Ravana, who had disturbed the sacrifices of the brahmanas and was harassing the demigods. Lord Krishna came to deliver the husband and wife pair of Vasudeva and Devaki, who had been imprisoned by Devaki's evil brother Kamsa. The character of each incarnation was different as well. Lord Narasimha was very ferocious and mercilessly killed Hiranyakashipu. Lord Rama was a great king who was completely devoted to dharma and righteousness. Lord Krishna was much more lenient as far as rules and regulations went, and was most merciful to His purest devotees, the gopis of Vrindavana.

God guides us based on our capacity to learn. The material world is made up of three distinct modes called *gunas*: goodness, passion, and ignorance. Vedic literature accounts for all these modes by having eighteen different Puranas, which are scriptures relating to ancient Vedic stories. There are six Puranas for each mode. In this way, even if a person is in the mode ignorance, someone who has no desire to learn about God, even that person has a chance to advance spiritually. For example, meat eating is prohibited for the people in the mode of goodness. However, meat eating is very difficult to give up for people living in the mode of ignorance. Thus the Puranas recommend the process of animal sacrifice for such people in the hopes that they will think of God while eating meat. The hope is that as one constantly thinks about God, His spiritual understanding will increase and that he'll eventually give up the practice of animal sacrifice.

"Primarily, religion means to know God and to love Him. That is religion...if I profess to follow some religion but I do not know who God is or how to love Him, I am practicing a cheating religion." (Shrila Prabhupada, Science of Self-Realization, Ch 1b)

Just because we see different forms of God with different accompanying scriptures, doesn't mean He is a figment of our imaginations. God is very real, and we should take advantage of this human form of life to get to know and love Him. It is a common practice for people to attend church and ask God to "give us our daily bread". While this sentiment is nice, God is already providing food to millions of animals who don't have the capacity to worship Him. God supplies us with all of our necessities. We should strive to reach a higher platform of worship. Instead of asking from God, we should give to Him. That is true love. If we offer our daily bread, or other food that He's been so kind to give us, then we gradually elevate ourselves to the platform of loving God. That is real religion.

"The supreme occupation, or dharma, for all humanity is that by which men can attain to loving devotional service unto the transcendent Lord. Such devotional service must be unmotivated and uninterrupted in order to completely satisfy the self." (Shrimad Bhagavatam, 1.2.6)

We may see many different rituals, and different processes for spiritual advancement, but the best religion is that which teaches us to love God. In this age, Lord Chaitanya inaugurated the sankirtana movement, the congregational chanting of the holy names of God, **"Hare Krishna Hare Krishna, Krishna Krishna Hare Hare, Hare Rama Hare Rama, Rama Rama, Hare Hare."** If we commit ourselves to chanting daily and following the process of devotional service, then we will surely see that God is one and that He is in everything and everyone.

Ishvara Parama Krishna

"Fools deride Me when I descend in the human form. They do not know My transcendental nature and My supreme dominion over all that be." (Lord Krishna, Bhagavad-gita, 9.11)

The internet revolution has brought about great advancements in the dissemination of information. We can quickly search for information on virtually any topic. This is generally a good thing, but it has its drawbacks as well.

According to Vedic teachings, knowledge of God should be heard through the process of disciplic succession, from someone who knows Lord Krishna. That person is the spiritual master, or the pure devotee of the Lord. The pure devotee spends all his time in devotional service to Krishna, thus the Lord reveals Himself to such a person. The devotee has no other interest than to please Krishna, so thus he is the proper person to go to. There are many other mundane scholars who study the Bhagavad-gita and come up with their own concocted theories about Krishna. Some say that He is just an ordinary human being, while others say that the Gita's teachings are merely symbolic and not to be taken literally. Such people can be classified as atheists.

The internet provides freedom of access, allowing anyone and everyone to publish their thoughts and ideas. One of the drawbacks to this is that one can find conflicting and contradictory information on the internet on matters relating to religion and Krishna. Shankaracharya instituted the Mayavada, or impersonalist, philosophical interpretation of the Vedas in the late eighth century, and that philosophy has gained widespread popularity ever since. Thus the internet is filled information and opinions along this line, i.e. that God is impersonal and that the point of human life is to study Vedanta and hopefully one day merge into the impersonal effulgence known as the *brahmajyoti*.

"Everyone serves the purpose of the Supreme Godhead, and what to speak of such small and insignificant living entities as ourselves? We are surely eternal servants of the Lord. The Mayavada philosophy maintains that the demigods, the living entities and the Supreme Personality of Godhead are all equal. It is therefore a most foolish misrepresentation of Vedic knowledge." (Shrila Prabhupada, Chaitanya Charitamrita, Adi 7.157 Purport)

Mayavadis tend to think that each of us are personal Gods, and that the Supreme Absolute Truth is an impersonal energy, called Brahman. They take Lord Krishna and His various incarnations to be human beings or regular living entities, products subject to the spell of maya. The Lord describes the foolishness of such people in the Bhagavad-gita, yet if one does internet searches on Lord Krishna or Lord Rama, one will encounter many such teachings of the Mayavadis. Some people even go so far as to criticize the activities of Krishna, focusing especially on His dancing with the gopis in the *rasa-lila*. The pastimes of Krishna are detailed in the tenth canto of the Shrimad Bhagavatam. Many people ignore what is contained in the rest of the book, namely that Krishna is God, and instead cherry-pick certain things which they can use to criticize the Lord.

Lord Chaitanya warned us to stay away from such philosophy and try not to even hear it at all. He believed that one who was instructed in the ways of the Mayavada philosophy would have a very difficult time coming to the platform of love for Krishna.

"Vyasadeva composed the Vedanta-sutra to deliver the conditioned souls from this material world, but Shankaracharya, by presenting the Vedanta-sutra in his own way, has clearly done a great disservice to human society, for one who follows his Mayavada philosophy is doomed. In the Vedanta-sutra, devotional service is clearly indicated, but the Mayavadi philosophers refuse to accept the spiritual body of the Supreme Absolute Person and refuse to accept that the living entity has an individual existence separate from that of the Supreme Lord. Thus they have created atheistic havoc all over the world, for such a conclusion is against the very nature of the transcendental process of pure devotional service. The Mayavadi philosophers' unrealizable ambition to become one with the Supreme through denying the existence of the Personality of Godhead results in a most calamitous misrepresentation of spiritual knowledge, and one who follows this philosophy is doomed to remain perpetually in this material world." (Shrila Prabhupada, Chaitanya Charitamrita, Adi 7.114 Purport)

People are naturally inclined to think of God as being personal; someone we should worship and be devoted to. By reading about or hearing the Mayavada philosophy, one is taken away from their natural inclination to know and love God. Even for those who are already devoted, reading such philosophy can be very depressing. We all love our parents and we never like it when others criticize them. In the same way, Krishna is our original father, and seeing Him treated as an ordinary human being is very offensive. The mind should be purified by thinking good thoughts.

The internet represents one of the most advanced forms of communication, so we should take advantage of this medium to disseminate the truth about Krishna. God is very nice to us, so we should be equally kind to Him by using everything at our disposal to distribute His Mercy to everyone. If we hear the truth about Krishna and lovingly serve Him, then no contradictory philosophy can ever touch us.

The Simple Life

"Undoubtedly I shall always live upon roots and fruits, living with you always I shall not bring about your affliction." (Sita Devi speaking to Lord Rama, Valmiki Ramayana, Ayodhya Kand, Sec 27)

Not too long ago, the majority of the labor force in America belonged to the agriculture sector. Farming for subsistence and profit was the primary occupation of most. Long hours were spent each day planting and harvesting crops, feeding and cleaning up after the farm animals, and then cooking and eating the three meals of the day. Sometimes conditions would be very tough and bountiful harvests weren't always guaranteed. Some years families would struggle and they would prosper in others. All in all, life was still very simple.

Fast forward to today, and almost no one is involved in the agriculture business. Technological advancements have increased farm productivity greatly, requiring far fewer farmers. America's crop production is so bountiful that the government actually pays farmers to not grow food as a means of controlling prices. As a result of this advancement, food is very readily available to all and a majority of the population is concerned with dieting and losing weight. Fine dining at expensive restaurants, fast food joints, and giant sized supermarkets mean that we have our pick as to what we want to eat and how much we will intake. Most of us now overindulge in eating and as a result, our government has declared an obesity epidemic. One need only watch television for a few minutes a day to find all the latest exercise gadgets and diet fads geared at reducing weight. Though we may be successful at times at losing weight through these methods, we generally gain it all back since we have difficulty sticking to exercise regimens and fanatic diets.

According to Vedic philosophy, the tongue and genitals are the hardest organs to control. One who is able to conquer the urge to overeat and indulge in illicit sex life is rewarded with peace of mind, allowing one to make progress in spiritual understanding. When Lord Rama, Krishna's incarnation in the Treta Yuga, was banished to the forest for fourteen years by His father Maharaja Dashratha, His wife Sita Devi wanted to accompany Him. According to the Vedic system, schooling occurs at the home of a spiritual master, known as the gurukula. Under the direction of the guru, boys living a celibate lifestyle, are taught about spiritual matters, including how to control one's eating. Students at the gurukula, known as brahmacharis, would beg from door to door to collect alms which would be given to the guru. The guru would then disperse this food amongst his students. If a student didn't receive any food, it was understood that he would have to fast until the next day or whenever the guru would provide him food. This system of austerity taught the students how to regulate their eating habits.

When Sita Devi was making her case to Lord Rama as to why she should be allowed to come to the forest with Him, she made it a point to say that she would gladly live upon "roots and fruits" during the exile period. Sita Devi was raised in the kingdom of Maharaja Janaka of Mithila from her childhood and was thus accustomed to eating the most sumptuous foods. Women would not attend school during that time, so she had no formal training in regulating her eating habits. Yet she was more than willing to give up all rich and good tasting food for the rest of her life in order to please her husband. This is the symptom of a person infused with pure love for God. Lord Rama was God Himself, and Sita Devi was completely devoted to Him. Devotees will undergo any amount of penance and austerity to make the Lord happy. In fact, this life is meant for *tapasya*, the voluntary acceptance of austerities aimed at delivering spiritual advancement. Lord Krishna says in the Bhagavad-gita,

"There is no possibility of one's becoming a yogi, O Arjuna, if one eats too much, or eats too little, sleeps too much or does not sleep enough." (Bg. 6.16)

Only one who has their senses regulated can raise themselves to the platform of love of God. If we have our senses in control, then we can realize Krishna is within us as the Supersoul, and thus we can always enjoy the bliss that comes with His association.

"My dear Lord, only by Your mercy and grace can the living entity get the human form of life, which is a chance to get out of the miserable condition of material existence. However, a person who possesses a human body but who cannot bring the senses under control is carried away by the waves of sensual enjoyment. As such, he cannot take shelter of Your lotus feet and thus engage in Your devotional service. The life of such a person is very unfortunate, and anyone living such a life of darkness is certainly cheating himself and thus cheating others also." (Lord Shiva, Krishna, The Supreme Personality of Godhead, Vol 2, Ch 8)

Sita Devi, though belonging to the woman class, whom the Vedas consider as having a lower birth along with vaishyas and shudras, had her senses completely under control, and was thus allowed to accompany Lord Rama to the forest. This proves that pure devotees can transcend any and all material designations. One may be a man, woman, brahmana, or shudra, but these classifications are only for people who haven't attained a pure love for Krishna. The Vedas allow such people to make gradual spiritual advancement by following the prescribed dharma for their specific class. However, *bhagavata-dharma*, pure devotional service to Krishna, is the highest form of worship and is available to everyone, even the animals. Thus Sita Devi was more than just the perfect woman, she was the perfect devotee.

Falling On Hard Times

"One who cannot deliver his dependents from the path of repeated birth and death should never become a spiritual master, a father, a husband, a mother or a worshipable demigod." (Rishabhadeva, Shrimad Bhagavatam 5.5.18)

The U.S. economy has fallen on hard times lately. The gross domestic product, GDP, has been shrinking instead of growing. The unemployment rate is very high and the stock market has completely tanked since last fall. This has caused the government to feverishly adopt new plans as a means of stimulating the economy.

The Obama administration came up with a plan along with the help of the Congress. A massive spending bill consisting of thousand of earmarks, the proponents said this would give the economy the jumpstart that it needed. Another similar bill was also passed last year by the Bush administration. Both bills have proved to do little to nothing to stimulate the economy.

"'This recession might linger for years,' President Barack Obama wrote in a Feb. 8 Washington Post op-ed. 'Our economy will lose 5 million more jobs. Unemployment will approach double digits. Every day, our economy gets sicker.' This was the justification for haste in passing Obama's stimulus package. Now, six months later, with just 10 percent of the $787 billion package spent, ordinary Americans don't think it's working.

Fifty-seven percent told the Gallup organization that the package has had no effect or has made the economy worse. Eighty-one percent believe that it has not benefitted them personally in the short run and 70 percent believe it will not benefit them in the long run. This opinion is not without factual basis. Unemployment reached 9.5 percent in June, with nearly 3 million jobs lost since Obama's op-ed. In July, it dipped to 9.4 percent, not because more jobs had been created, but because only 242,000 jobs were lost and some 400,000 individuals stopped looking for work and ceased to count as 'unemployed.'" (Editorial, San Francisco Examiner, Aug 18, 2009)

Taking a close look at how economics works, one can understand the flaw in such proposals. Our economic system is considered to be a free market one. Goods and services are exchanged peaceably and voluntarily between people along with a respect for property rights and the rule of law. Government's role in this system is to ensure that the exchanges are in fact voluntary, and that contracts and agreements are honored. If the market is left on its own, with government playing its minimal role, growth will occur naturally through the forces of competition. This has proved to be the case time and time again throughout the country's history. From 1980 to 2001, the government did little to stimulate economic activity in the form of subsidies or other hand outs, and the result was that the U.S. economy grew at an unprecedented rate. Prior to that, recessions were very common, with GDP rates fluctuating up and down in the 1970s.

"Just as one who cuts off the udders of a cow with the hope of getting milk never acquires it, so also a state in which taxes are levied inappropriately, thus harassing the subjects, does not prosper." (Mahabharata, 12.71.16)

According to the Vedas, the material world is made up of three *gunas* or modes: goodness, passion, and ignorance. The free market system is the embodiment of the mode of passion. People, through their buying and selling habits, are striving for fruitive results. The stock market is a great example of this; traders frantically buying and selling, all in hopes of turning a profit. When people are left to compete with one another, the mode of passion kicks in and economic circumstances improve as a result.

This isn't a new idea. According the Mahabharata, a book written about five thousand years ago, a king should make sure that taxes are low for vaishyas, the mercantile class of people. The reason for this is that if taxes are high, the producers will have no incentive to produce. That will mean less money coming in to the treasury. Not only should taxes be low, but the treasury should spend money wisely and for legitimate purposes.

"The treasury of a king is meant for the protection of the army, his subjects and of righteousness (Dharma). If it is used for these purposes, it will prove beneficial. On the other hand, if the treasury is misused, it will prove disastrous. Should the king use the royal treasury for his wife and children and to fulfill his own sensual pursuits, it will bring him unhappiness and he will attain hell." (Shukraniti 4.2.3-5, taken from Purpose and Function of Government According to Mahabharata)

Contrast this with today's leaders and their policies. The recent stimulus packages are nothing more than the taking of money from one group of people, the producers, and transferring it to another group, the non-producers. Such a plan is destined to fail.

So why the sudden downturn in the economy? As with any system based on the mode of passion, the health of an economy will always go through ups and downs. The same way that some business fail and others succeed, the economy is not guaranteed to grow every quarter of every year. Though things look bleak now, objectively speaking, the standard of life in America has never been better. Even with a bad economy, every material comfort is at our fingertips. Keeping this mind, the government should shift its focus to more important areas. According to the Vedas, a person should not be a king or a leader unless he can deliver his dependents from the cycle of birth and death. Whether the economy is good or bad, the soul is eternal. If we do not train ourselves to always be thinking about God, then we will be forced to accept another body after this life. A government's primary duty should be to elevate people to the mode of goodness by providing them spiritual guidance. The opportunity today is great since such knowledge is almost completely absent in society.

The best spiritual education in this age comes from chanting the holy names of God, "**Hare Krishna Hare Krishna, Krishna Krishna, Hare Hare, Hare Rama Hare Rama, Rama Rama, Hare Hare.**" This is the beginning of spiritual life and it costs nothing. Chanting pays dividends higher than any stock or government stimulus plan. If our consciousness is always linked with the Supreme Lord, then nothing, including a recession, can hurt us.

Food For The Soul

"The whole material world is full of hungry living beings. The hunger is not for good food, shelter or sense gratification. The hunger is for the spiritual atmosphere." (Shrila Prabhupada, Shrimad Bhagavatam, 1.12.6 Purport)

A staple of the dining out experience in America is the buffet restaurant. America is the "land of the free and the home of the brave", and thus there is increased freedom in all aspects of life, especially in eating. Dining out at a buffet restaurant provides a one-of-a-kind eating experience, with no menus to look at and no time spent waiting for food to be brought to your table.

At a normal restaurant, we have to look over the menu and figure what we want to eat. It's usually a tough decision because there's probably more than one thing on the menu that would satisfy our taste buds. We have to be really careful because if we choose the wrong dish, we're stuck with it unless we want to fork over more money for something else. A buffet lets us hedge our bet. All the food is already out there for us to choose from. With the "all you can eat" pricing model, it is in our interest to stuff ourselves until we can't eat any more so that we can get the biggest bang for our buck.

A buffet meal is best enjoyed on an empty stomach. If we have advance notice prior to going to a buffet restaurant, we strategize ahead by altering our eating schedule accordingly. It is also for this reason that many restaurants serve buffets only on weekends as part of brunch, a meal considered as either a late breakfast or an early lunch. Most people wake up later on the weekends, so brunch represents their first meal of the day, a time when they are usually quite hungry.

The goal is to make sure we are as hungry as we can possibly be when we arrive at the restaurant. Even while eating, we may try different techniques so as to trick ourselves into still being hungry. One of the more common strategies is to stay away from soda and other beverages, so as to leave more room in the stomach. In the South, some people even go as far as jumping off toilets in the restrooms as a means of "making room" in the stomach. The hungrier we are, the more food we will be able to intake and the more we will enjoy it, or so we think. This theory applies to all areas of sense enjoyment. The less we have of something, the more we appreciate it. "Don't know what you've got til it's gone" as the saying goes.

According to the Vedas, this current age is known as Kali Yuga, meaning the age of quarrel and hypocrisy. In Kali Yuga, religion is almost non-existent, with dharma existing at only one quarter its full strength. Even the religions that do exist today are mostly cheating ones, advising people to do everything except love God. Because of this deficiency, God has made the path of self-realization much easier in this age. Lord Krishna Himself came to this earth some five hundred years ago in the form of Lord Chaitanya to initiate the sankirtana movement. Sankirtana is the process of congregationally chanting the holy names of God, **"Hare Krishna Hare Krishna, Krishna Krishna, Hare Hare, Hare Rama Hare Rama, Rama Rama Hare Hare."** Lord Chaitanya taught us that in this age, there is no other way of realizing God besides constantly chanting His name:

"In this age of quarrel and disagreement, the Kali Yuga, there is no other way of spiritual realization but this chanting of the names. There is no other way, there is no other way, there is no other way." (Chaitanya Charitamrita, Adi 17.21)

This method of self realization may seem very simple, but it is effective due to our lack of religious awareness. Fortunately for us, we are all hungry for spiritual knowledge and this lack of education has actually made us hungrier for serving Krishna, even if we may not realize it. Our current activities involving meat eating, intoxication, gambling, and illicit sex life which are all attempts at pleasing the senses and achieving everlasting peace and happiness. However, since these are all on the material platform, they never succeed in fulfilling our desires and thus we remain searching after that one thing that can make us truly happy.

"...as a hungry man cannot be made happy by all comforts of life minus foodstuff, so the hungry man for eternal Absolute Happiness cannot be detracted by any amount of material happiness." (Shrila Prabhupada, Shrimad Bhagavatam, 1.13.17 Purport)

Those who take to chanting the holy names of the Lord immediately appreciate it since it is a religious activity that actually delivers real benefits. Chanting becomes the most attractive religious activity because we immediately get connected with Krishna. Through chanting our interest in God is spurred on, and we gradually take to the other processes of devotional service.

Eating at a buffet is a fun experience, but the aftermath can be quite painful. Heartburn, indigestion, or extreme fatigue usually follows such a heavy meal. Unlike eating at a buffet, chanting God's name has no negative side effects.

"You'll find happiness. If you chant Hare Krishna twenty-four hours, you'll never get tired, and that is the... You'll never get tired. In any other material thing, if you chant or you repeat three times, you'll get tired. It is practical test. But if you go on chanting Hare Krishna twenty-four hours, you'll never get tired. So if you engage yourself in the activity of Krishna consciousness, you'll never get tired because you are acting on the spiritual platform. Spiritual platform is absolute. The material platform is different. If you work very hard, then you get tired." (Shrila Prabhupada, Lecture, New York, Sep 2, 1966)

The more we do it, the more we become attracted to it. So let us all take advantage of this great gift given to us by Lord Chaitanya, and we'll be satisfying our real hunger.

Giving To The Lord

"(Those) who rejoice to see another's prosperity and are sore distressed at their misfortune; to whom, O Rama, You are dear as their own lives, in their hearts be Your blessed abode." (Maharishi Valmiki speaking to Lord Rama, Ramacharitamanasa)

According to Vedic philosophy there are three kinds of miseries in this material world. *Adhidaivic* miseries are those brought on by nature, such as hurricanes, earthquakes, tornadoes, etc. *Adhyatmic* refers to miseries brought about by physical and mental ailments. Taking birth in the material world means that we are eventually bound to catch some disease or another. Many times our mind can cause us ailments as well, through excessive hankering and lamenting. The third kind of misery, known as *adhibhautic*, is that brought about by other living entities. These miseries can come from animals such as insects who bite us, or other human beings who may torment us.

Though one may sometimes derive pleasure from mocking and annoying others, such behavior isn't considered proper. In the Ramacharitamanasa of Tulsidas, Maharishi Valmiki beautifully elaborates on the qualities of a devotee. One thing that he mentions is that devotees of God always feel bad when others are in distress and feel good when others are happy. Envy is a quality that we all possess to some degree, so it is not surprising if we sometimes feel happy at the miseries of others. We think to ourselves, "Oh good, I'm not the only one who isn't happy all the time. It's good that they found out just how hard life can be." This sort of behavior is very immature because another's fortunes or misfortunes actually have no effect on us. A truly saintly person is one who sees everyone on an equal footing. According to Lord Krishna, a devotee even has compassion for a dog and a dog-eater:

"The humble sage, by virtue of true knowledge, sees with equal vision a learned and gentle brahmana, a cow, an elephant, a dog and a dog-eater [outcaste] ." (Bhagavad-gita, 5.18)

When Sita Devi, the wife of Lord Rama, was pleading with her husband to allow her to accompany Him to the forest for fourteen years, she made it a point to tell Him that she would not cause Him any afflictions while in the forest.

"Undoubtedly I shall always live upon roots and fruits, living with you always I shall not bring about your affliction." (Valmiki Ramayana, Ayodhya Kand, Sec 27)

Lord Rama, God Himself, was ordered to live in the forest by His father Maharaja Dashratha, the king of Ayodhya. Being married at the time, the Lord wanted His wife to remain at home where she would be protected. Maintaining a wife is not an easy task for a husband, even in the most perfect of conditions. During that time, the Treta Yuga, forest life was meant only for people in the renounced order of life, sannyasis. It would have been very difficult to protect Sita while living in such austere conditions. The Vedic injunction is that a wife must be protected at all times by the husband, and she is to be looked after with the same attention as one would give to a child. It is for this reason that the Lord wanted Sita to remain in the kingdom for the duration of the exile period.

Sita Devi, however, was the incarnation of the goddess of fortune, Lakshmi. Lakshmi is the wife of Lord Narayana, who is God Himself residing in the spiritual world. If one comes across paintings or photos of Lakshmi-Narayana, one will often see Lakshmi massaging the feet of a resting Lord Narayana. It is not that the wife is treated as a servant. That would be missing the meaning behind such a scene. The constitutional position of all living entities is to serve God, but this fact is only realized after one makes steady progress in the execution of devotional service. Sita Devi, being a pure a devotee of God, always wanted to serve her *pati* or Lord, and it is for this reason that Rama allowed her to do so by eventually acquiescing to her request. God is very nice in that he voluntarily enters into loving relationships with His devotees based on their desires. Sometimes God will assume the form of a son, a husband, or even a lover simply to satisfy His devotees.

From Sita Devi's example, we can learn the proper method of devotional service. Obviously God is purely spiritual, so He is not capable of suffering any afflictions. Still, our attitude should be that we shouldn't needlessly bother the Lord for material things.

"One should render transcendental loving service to the Supreme Lord Krishna favorably and without desire for material profit or gain through fruitive activities or philosophical speculation. That is called pure devotional service." (Shrila Rupa Goswami, *Bhakti-rasamrta-sindhu*)

Instead of repeatedly asking *from* the Lord, we should give *to* Him. By constantly chanting His name, reading His books, serving the lotus of feet of His devotees, and offering Him prayers, we can offer all our thoughts, words, and deeds as a sacrifice to the Lord. In return, He rewards us with eternal devotion to Him, which is the greatest boon in life.

Spreading The Message

"Just as a radio broadcasts mundane news, the bona fide guru broadcasts the news from Vaikuntha." (Shrila Prabhupada, Shrimad Bhagavatam, 11.3.21, Purport)

Recently on CNN, a television cable news network, a story was done providing people tips on how to purchase a health insurance plan. Shown during the afternoon, the idea appeared to have great potential, but the story didn't live up to it.

CNN, known as the Cable News Network, was the pioneer in the cable television news genre. Prior to its founding in 1980, the only source for national news on television was what was shown on the big three television networks: ABC, NBC, and CBS. Walter Cronkite became a household name as the anchor of the CBS evening news in the 1960s and early 1970s. Usually shown between the hours of 6 and 7 pm, the nightly television newscasts always garnered huge ratings. CNN tapped into this market by dedicating an entire cable channel to strictly showing news. Thus, the 24 hour news cycle began. In the last 15 years or so, cable news has really taken off with new networks such as FOX and MSNBC joining the ranks. All these channels display news tickers at the bottom of the screen throughout the day, scrolling through the latest headlines. Much of the content on these channels has become formulaic. The typical news hour consists of an anchor reading the latest news headlines, followed by panels of experts and guests discussing the topics. Many times the guests are on opposing sides of an issue, so debates naturally ensue. Other segments, such as do-it-yourself guides and helpful hints for consumers, are also quite common on cable news networks. CNN had one such segment recently dedicated to the issue of health insurance and how people can go about buying it.

Having health insurance is very important for people living in America. With the increase in government mandates and regulation over employers, hospitals and doctors, it is almost a necessity to have some sort of health insurance versus paying for medical expenses out-of-pocket. A health insurance plan can be very complicated, with all sorts of benefits, limits on out-of-pocket expenses, and deductibles. For example, one insurance plan may cover hospital visits completely, while others require the patient to pay a certain amount per day of hospital confinement, up to a certain maximum amount. A typical health insurance plan divides its benefits summary into categories such as preventive care, outpatient care, allergy care, hospital care, emergency car, maternity care, home health care, etc. An insurance company is in business for one reason, to make money. The customer, on the other hand, wants to spend as little money as possible and still get good coverage. With these forces colliding, along with issues of competition, malpractice insurance, in-network versus out-of-network, it is quite understandable to think that some people could use some guidance on which plans are the best ones for them.

The story on CNN however, didn't provide any useful information at all. A health insurance "expert" appeared as a guest and suggested that people shop around for the best health insurance plan. People were also urged to look for plans with a low deductible. These tips were well-intentioned but most people already know all of this. People don't need to be told how to shop around or how to look for low prices. When acting in their own self-interest, people will automatically buy things that are suited to their needs. Some value price over quality and others vice versa. In a free society, these things take care of themselves. No one is taught how to purchase a cell phone plan, a flat screen television, or even shop for groceries. People buy what they want and at the price they are willing to pay.

The CNN story is indicative of a larger problem with the news media. They tend to look down at their audience and give them useless information. They also devote much airtime to praising celebrities, detailing their every move. While this might be entertaining to some, the knowledge received is very little and has no lasting value.

"There are so many departments in a university: technological, medical, engineering, etc. But where is the department to know and understand what this life is, what God is, and what our relationship is?" (Shrila Prabhupada)

The twenty-four cable networks have a real opportunity to teach people about meaningful topics, such as the soul and its relationship with God. Spiritual education is seriously lacking in this age. We spend twelve years in school and then four plus years in college studying various material subjects. We learn about the ins and outs of various sciences and how to read and write, but the science of the soul is never taught.

The news media reaches millions of people daily, so if they spent even five minutes out of every hour discussing a verse from the Bhagavad-gita or other Vedic scriptures, then society would be greatly benefitted. Instead of live debates with Republican and Democrat strategists, they could show clips of Shrila Prabhupada speeches and have discussions on them. The Vedic literature is so vast that it never gets tiring to listen to. In India during the 1980s, television serials devoted to the Mahabharata and the Ramayana were shown and the people tuned in by the millions. In America, Mel Gibson's *The Passion of the Christ* movie set records at the box office. This proves that the desire for spiritual education is there. It is in the financial interest of these news organizations to fulfill that desire. If you show it, they will come.

The Power of Love

"Devotional service alone is competent to award a devotee all material power. A pure devotee, however, is never attached to material power, although he gets it very easily without personal endeavor." (Shrila Prabhupada, Shrimad Bhagavatam, **6.16.28 Purport)**

Every person wants to attain some type of power. The material world consists of three subtle elements: mind, intelligence, and false ego. It is this ego that causes one to crave attention in the form of fame and fortune which come as a result of the acquisition of some sort of power or perfection in a certain field.

Since the material world means a place where material qualities exist, known as *gunas*, each person has different desires. In fact, that is the definition of karma, i.e. work performed with desire for fruitive results. Karma is the cause of our being in this material world and it is also the determining factor of the type of body we will have in the next life. Some people seek power in the form of yogic *siddhis*. We are all familiar with the term yoga, which we generally associate with the hatha yoga system involving various breathing exercises and sitting postures. Yoga actually means to have union of the soul with Krishna, or God. The hatha-yoga system was created as a way to allow those who are overly attached to their senses to be able to break free of them. This system naturally has very nice side effects, among which are the yogic siddhis. Siddhi means a perfection or an extraordinary power, and by practicing this type of yoga very strictly and sincerely one can gain such powers as being able to become infinitesimally small (*anima*), being able to travel to various planets at the speed of the mind, and being able to determine the time of one's death. The full list is delineated in the Vedic scriptures.

One doesn't have to a yogi to crave material power. Bodybuilders train very hard to be able to have a physique which they can show off in magazines and on videos. They strive to be able to lift very heavy weights, wanting to bench-press more than anyone else in their field. Politicians are some of the more well-known seekers of power. In today's political scene, it is more and more common to find that the people who run for office are already millionaires in their private life. Having amassed large amounts of money, they still aren't satisfied and thus they look to politics as a means of acquiring even more power. Once they get into office, they have a very difficult time giving up the post. In New York City, Mayor Michael Bloomberg recently got the legislature to change an existing law that would have limited his term in office. He is now free to run for mayor again. These term-limit laws were enacted by the public as a way of preventing one person from amassing too much power by remaining in office indefinitely. The first president of the United States, George Washington, voluntarily stepped down after serving two terms, a tradition which was honored for almost one hundred fifty years after that. However, during the early 1930s, President Franklin Delano Roosevelt was elected to office for an unprecedented four terms. So unwilling to give up his position, he eventually died in office. Congress subsequently passed the twenty-second amendment to the Constitution which now limits presidents to serving only two terms.

On the surface, acquiring powers or other perfections in material endeavors may not seem like a bad thing. We all have to do something with our time after all, for the mind must always be active. We all must be engaged in some activity or another, and striving to achieve our goals is a good way to stay occupied. The problem is that these material perfections are all temporary. One may acquire a massive amount of wealth, but that money doesn't come with us after we die. We may be a great big politician loved and adored by all, but that can all be taken away in a second, as we saw with Mahatma Gandhi. Not only are these acquisitions of power only temporary, but they also require great effort to secure. Bodybuilders spend hours and hours in the gym torturing themselves by lifting heavy weights. In fact, the proper technique for increasing the mass of the body muscles is to actually hurt them by lifting heavier and heavier weights. The muscles eventually grow as a result of being pushed to the limit. Yogic *siddhis* are similarly difficult to acquire. One must go to a secluded place, concentrating the mind very seriously on the Supreme Lord for long periods of time. The rules and regulations are very strict.

And what does one gain from these perfections? According to the Vedas, this human form of life is meant for God realization. Any activity which helps us achieve this goal is worthwhile, and anything that takes us further away from God is considered a waste of time. In actuality, one doesn't have to work very hard to achieve all these material perfections, for they come naturally to those who engage themselves in devotional service. Technically known as bhakti yoga, devotional service is the discipline of dovetailing all of one's activities with the desires of the Supreme Lord Krishna. One may wonder what these activities entail. They can be anything actually. One can be singing and thinking of God. One can even be eating nice food and thinking of God. There are nine distinct processes of bhakti yoga, as outlined by Prahlada Maharaja: hearing, chanting, remembering, worshiping, serving the lotus feet of the Lord, offering prayers, carrying out the orders of the Lord, becoming friends with Him, and surrendering everything to Him. One can attain perfection of life by only engaging in one of these processes.

Lord Hanuman is a great example of someone who acquired tremendous power simply as a result of serving the Lord. Born as a Vanara, a monkey with human-like characteristics, Hanuman had tremendous power that he was completely unaware of. Having had his jaw broken in his youth by the demigod Indra, Hanuman was completely pious and devoted to God but he had no recollection of his immense strength. However, when the time came to serve Lord Rama, God Himself, Hanuman became reacquainted with his strength. He had the power to make himself larger than a mountain and to fly through the air with the speed of the wind, for he was the son of the wind god, Vayu. Hanuman could also assume any shape at will, which was similar to a power possessed by Rakshasa demons. However, Hanuman used all these powers for one purpose, to rescue Sita Devi, Lord Rama's wife, from the clutches of Ravana. A Rakshasa demon of a terrible nature, Ravana had kidnapped Sita from the forest while Rama and His brother Lakshmana were not around. His kingdom was on the island of Lanka and Hanuman was the one deputed to find Sita and bring back the details of her whereabouts to Lord Rama. Aside from finding Sita, Hanuman playfully set fire to the city of Lanka and also served as the chief warrior in Lord Rama's fight against Ravana and his band of Rakshasas. Rama proved victorious and he awarded Hanuman with eternal devotion to Him. To this day, Hanuman is synonymous with love and devotion to Lord Rama, and also strength and courage in one's religious endeavors.

Attaining perfections and acquiring power is not prohibited according to the Vedas, but it just needs to be used for the right purpose. Hanuman was never puffed up with his power, for he viewed himself as a humble servant of the Lord. This is the example to follow. The only thing required from us is that we be sincere in our devotional service. Seeing that, God will automatically provide us all the necessary tools to serve Him properly.

Rules of Etiquette

"The devotees of the Lord are released from all kinds of sins because they eat food which is offered first for sacrifice. Others, who prepare food for personal sense enjoyment, verily eat only sin." (Lord Krishna, Bhagavad-gita, 3.13)

Depending on the customs and norms of a specific society, there are certain rules of etiquette that are generally followed. Attending formal wedding receptions, tipping a waiter at a restaurant, and even in playing sports, rules of etiquette dictate our behavior in a wide range of social environments.

In America for example, it customary to bring cash gifts to a wedding. The attendees try to estimate the cost incurred to the host for their food and beverage at the wedding. The amount of the cash gift should be equal to or greater than this cost. When dining out at a restaurant, one is expected to leave a gratuity to the waiter of an amount between fifteen to twenty percent of the total bill. When playing the sport of tennis, players raise their hand up and apologize for points won through good luck, such as a miss-hit or the ball hitting the net cord.

These are just some of the examples of standard etiquette and there are many more associated with all sorts of activities. The one thing all these rules have in common is that they are all voluntarily implemented. No one is required to leave a tip in a restaurant or hold a door open for someone else. Yet the majority of society follows these rules. The reason they are followed is that human beings naturally have a tendency to serve. Etiquette represents a way for us to serve our fellow man and to show respect to others. By voluntarily abiding by them, we are thinking outside of our own desires, and giving attention to the feelings of others. Such activity naturally purifies us, since we are happiest when we are acting unselfishly.

The Vedas, the ancient books of knowledge originating in India, have many rules and regulations relating to etiquette. People living in the householder stage of life, known as *grihastha*, are obligated to serve the members of the other orders of society. Householders are involved in fruitive activity to procure wealth, religiosity, and sense gratification. While there is nothing wrong with earning a living, the Vedas teach a householder to use that wealth for spiritual advancement. For example, when eating, a householder is advised to first offer food to God, and then to distribute that food to the guests of the house. Only after the guests have finished eating is the householder allowed to eat whatever remains. It is also the standard etiquette that the wife and other women in the family don't eat until after the male members have finished. Those growing up in Hindu families are very familiar with this custom. When attending family gatherings, one will often see all the women huddled together in the kitchen and the men together in a separate room. When it comes time to eat, the children and elderly are served first, followed by the men, with the women eating after everyone has finished. It takes much cajoling from the men to get the women to eat with them, for the women are very hesitant to break with tradition.

Such a system isn't chauvinistic, but it is a means for creating a happy family life. According to the Vedas, the wife serves the husband, and the husband protects the wife. This leads to a peaceful life, leaving time for spiritual advancement. The wife shares whatever spiritual merits her husband accumulates, thus it is in her interest to see the husband succeed in his endeavors.

Sita Devi, the wife of Lord Rama, who was God Himself, was very well acquainted with these rules of etiquette pertaining to husband-wife relations. Aside from being an incarnation of Goddess Lakshmi, the wife of Lord Narayana, Sita was raised in the kingdom of one of the most pious kings in history, Maharaja Janaka of Mithila. Though receiving no formal education in the Vedas, she was taught properly at home by her parents, which along with her inherent qualities, made her the perfect women. Her husband, Lord Rama, was ordered to live in the forest for fourteen years by His father King Dashratha. Instead of remaining home as Lord Rama had asked her to do, Sita insisted on following the Lord to the forest. As part of her plea, she informed Him that she would always walk before Him and take her meals only after He had eaten.

"Always I shall precede you when walking, and shall take my repast after you have taken it, willing am I to view mountains, rivulets, lakes, and ponds." (Valmiki Ramayana, Ayodhya Kand, Sec 27)

Aside from being proper etiquette for a wife, this also represents the rule that should be followed by devotees of God. Similar to the concept of saying grace, the Vedas teach us to offer our food to Krishna prior to eating. God is kind enough to provide us plenty of milk, fruits, and food grains for our survival. We should offer these foodstuffs to His deity prior to eating as a way of thanking Him. The Lord is so kind that He spiritually eats the food, but then leaves everything for us. The remaining food is known as prasadam, meaning the Lord's mercy.

Sita Devi's example is a very nice one to follow for devotees of the Lord. God is completely self-satisfied and requires nothing from us, but He gladly accepts anything offered to Him with love and devotion. Loving Krishna means following the highest standard of etiquette.

The Joys of Childhood

"In all activities just depend upon Me and work always under My protection. In such devotional service, be fully conscious of Me." (Lord Krishna, Bhagavad-gita, 18.57)

Most of us look back very fondly on our childhood. It was a time of care-free innocence where we didn't worry about much. When we weren't in school, we would spend all our time playing or having some sort of fun. We never really worried about anything.

When we become adults, we notice this same attitude reflected in the children that we meet. When out in a public setting, we always see children running around, talking to strangers, and breaking all the rules of social etiquette. For the most part, this behavior is excused by the adults because they understand the innocence of the child. Kids don't know any better, and they mean well. They aren't very self conscious and they view everyone as their friend.

"Chaitanya Mahaprabhu says that the actual identity of every living creature is that he is the eternal servant of God. If one thinks like that—'I am no one else's servant; my business is to serve God'—then he is liberated. His heart is immediately cleansed, and he is liberated. And after one has reached that, then all one's cares and anxieties in this world are over because one knows, 'I am a servant of God. God will give me protection. Why should I worry about anything?' It is just like a child. A child knows that his mother and father will take care of him. He is free. If he should go to touch fire, his mother will take care of him: 'Oh, my dear child, don't touch.' The mother is always looking after him. So why don't you put your trust in God? Actually, you are under the protection of God." (Shrila Prabhupada, Science of Self-Realization, Ch 8a)

The bliss that children feel is a result of knowing that their parents will always be there to protect them. A child doesn't worry about how he or she will eat dinner that night or whether they will have enough money to pay the bills. Their mother and father take care of everything, so they are free to enjoy life without any worries.

Though they are just children and don't have any understanding of the real world, adults can learn a lesson by observing their behavior. Now that we are older, we are more susceptible to be illusioned, one of the four defects of man. Man is subject to four primary defects: being easily illusioned, being prone to commit mistakes, having a propensity to cheat, and having imperfect senses. After finishing school and holding a steady job, we think ourselves the doers of everything. We gather worldly possessions and then start to worry about how we will maintain them. Living with our spouse and children can be one the more stressful stages of our life. Having children means constantly worrying about their safety and well-being. "Are my kids safe? Will I have enough money to support my family? Am I saving enough for them to be able to go to college?" On top of these worries, one has to manage the household affairs, keeping track of bills and expenditures, and making sure that the children are properly attending school and finishing their homework. It's a life full of worry. While we should definitely be concerned with the welfare of our family, we needn't be too worried about material affairs since God actually takes care of everything. Our constant hankering and lamenting is actually due to our forgetfulness of the relationship we have with God.

Lord Krishna, the Supreme Personality of Godhead, is our original father. He provides protection to all His devotees. It's just a matter of us realizing that He's there. If we recognize the fact that He's always looking after us, it will be much easier for us to approach Him. Through the process of devotional service, we can learn to become attached to Krishna, which will result in all our fears being vanquished. In the Bhagavad-gita, the Lord Himself says that we should practice devotion and make our minds transcendentally situated.

"One who is thus transcendentally situated at once realizes the Supreme Brahman. He never laments nor desires to have anything; he is equally disposed to every living entity. In that state he attains pure devotional service unto Me." (Lord Krishna, Bhagavad-gita, 18.54)

No more hankering and no more lamenting. Being fully conscious of God, our fears vanish. We return to the mindset that we had during our childhood and enjoy a blissful spiritual life. In this day and age, the best way to elevate our spiritual consciousness is to constantly chant the holy names of God, **"Hare Krishna Hare Krishna, Krishna Krishna, Hare Hare, Hare Rama Hare Rama, Rama Rama, Hare Hare"** It's so simple, even a child can do it.

Radhashtami 2009

123

"O Radha, you are dearer to me than my life even and I am like the same to you. There has been no point of separation or difference between us. Both of us have one and the same form." (Lord Krishna speaking to Radha just prior to their advent on earth, Brahmavaivarta Purana, Krishna-Janma Khand)

Radhashtami is the appearance day celebration of Shrimati Radharani, the eternal consort of Lord Krishna. Just as we take our spouse to be our partner for life, God has a life partner in His eternal consorts. Though He has different forms and incarnations such as Rama, Narasimha, Varaha, etc., according to the Brahmavaivarta, Vishnu, and Bhagavata Puranas, Krishna is the original form of God. Krishna's immediate expansion and pleasure potency is Radharani, often referred to just as Radha.

Radha is known as Krishna's pleasure potency, *hladini-shakti*. Krishna is the energetic and Radha is His energy, similar to the way wives are referred to as the better-half of their husbands. She is completely engrossed in thoughts of Krishna, loving Him purely and perfectly. Actually, it is not possible for one to love Krishna more than Radha does, for out of all the gopis, she is Krishna's favorite. Just as there are various forms of Krishna, so there exist many expansions of Radha. All the great demigoddesses and the various Lakshmis are all considered to emanate from her. Radhashtami is celebrated because it marks the anniversary of when she took birth on this earth some five thousand years ago.

Just like Krishna, Radha is eternal, so she technically doesn't take birth in the material world. For this reason, the occasion of her birth is referred to as her appearance day. According to the different Puranas, there are several versions of the story relating to the circumstances of her appearance. The reason for this is that God reenacts His pastimes on earth over and over again in the different *kalpas*, or creations. The general story is that Radha, Krishna, and their associates were enjoying their pastimes on the spiritual planet of Krishnaloka, when a misunderstanding arose between Radha and Krishna's friend Shridama over Krishna's playing with one of the gopis. As a result, Shridama cursed Radha to appear on earth and be separated from Krishna for one hundred years. This coincided with Krishna's appearance on earth, the purpose of which was to kill the demon Kamsa and to deliver His dependents. Naturally whenever God comes to earth, He brings His closest associates with him.

Radharani appeared fifteen days after Krishna did, as the daughter of Vrishabhanu and Kirtida.

"The birth of Radharani was not from the womb of any human being. She was found by her father in the field. While father was plowing, he saw one little nice child is lying there, and he had no children, so he caught it and presented to the queen, 'Oh, here we have got a very nice child.' 'How you got?' 'Oh, in the field.' Just see. Radharani's *janma* is like that." (Shrila Prabhupada, Lecture, Montreal, Aug. 30, 1968)

As the tradition goes, Radha actually didn't open her eyes for the first few days, a fact which worried her parents. They were concerned that she might be blind, so they invited the venerable Narada Muni to come and assess the situation. He was immediately taken aback after seeing Radha, for he knew she was no ordinary child. He advised Vrishabhanu not to worry and to hold an elaborate feast and invite Nanda and Yashoda, the foster-parents of Krishna. When baby Krishna came over, He crawled to Radha's crib to look at her. When she finally opened her eyes, Krishna was the first person she saw.

In their youth, the two enjoyed many wonderful pastimes in Vrindavana, but sadly the Lord would have to leave and finish His pastimes in Mathura and Dvaraka. Radha and the other gopis were left in Vrindavana always pining for the Lord. Such a separation may seem like a bad thing, but it actually brings about a pleasurable feeling. Worshiping the Lord in the mood of separation was the process recommended by Lord Chaitanya, for it is very blissful and arouses feelings of Krishna *prema*. Radhrani's separation anxiety was very great and she even declared that no one except Sita Devi, Lord Rama's wife, knew what she was experiencing.

"This type of grief was known either to Sita or to me. Compared to me, there is no one else in the three worlds whose mind is so painful. Can any woman believe in my pain after looking at me? Oh son Uddhava, what other women have faced such a type of grief? Among women, there is no one who is so badly suffering like Radha, who is suffering from separation from her Lord and is devoid of fortune and is completely grief-stricken. There is no one else among the damsels feeling more painful at heart than Radhika. In this universe the husband who happens to be the *kalpavriksha* (wish-fulfilling tree) was achieved by me, but I have been deprived of the same because of cruel destiny. With one look at His lotus-like feet as well as His moon-like face and His costumes, my birth and my life have become successful. With the hearing of whose name all the life airs become activated and sprout like flowers and the soul is filled with affection, the one who touched me at the time of conjugal pleasure and with that I enjoyed the glory of the three worlds. How can I forget such a lord by getting any amount of riches?" (Radharani speaking to Krishna's friend and envoy Uddhava, Brahmavaivarta Purana, Krishna-Janma Khand)

There is no difference between God and His name. Merely thinking of Him and reciting His name means we are in direct association with Him. In this way, there is actually never any separation between the Lord and His devotees. Devotees typically fast until noon on Radhashtami and then have discussions about Radha and Krishna. The best way to celebrate the grand pair is to always call chant their holy names found in the maha-mantra: **"Hare Krishna Hare Krishna,**

Krishna Krishna, Hare Hare, Hare Rama Hare Rama, Rama Rama, Hare Hare". *Krishna* is the original name of God and *Hare* refers to the Lord's energy in the form of Radha. Jai Shri Radhe!

Remover of Fears

"Being fearless in your company, Oh my intelligent husband and great hero, I shall behold on all sides ponds filled with wild geese and ducks and beautified with a collection of full-blown lotuses, and shall bathe there every day, pursuing the same vow with you..." (Sita Devi speaking to Lord Rama, Valmiki Ramayana, Ayodhya Kand, Sec 27)

At its core, animal life consists of eating, sleeping, mating and fearing. These four activities are evidenced in all animal species, from the aquatics all the way to human beings. Lions protecting their cubs from attackers, penguins protecting their eggs from the harsh cold, and human beings protecting their children are all examples of the mode of defense in action.

Human beings have a greater sense of intelligence than other animals, and a result, we tend to fear and defend more things than simply our immediate family. We develop attachment to our various material possessions, and we are constantly trying to protect them. In the modern age, the concept of insurance has arisen as a means of alleviating our fears. We have insurance to protect our cars, our homes, our health, and even our life. The advanced technological age has brought about an increase in material wealth and with that, an increase in the need to defend. Human beings fear things that they don't know or understand, and they also fear failing at their endeavors. The greatest fear of all is the fear of leaving this material world at the time of death.

So how does one alleviate these worries? According to Vedic philosophy, knowledge is the ultimate weapon in our battle against fear.

"A faithful man who is absorbed in transcendental knowledge and who subdues his senses quickly attains the supreme spiritual peace." (Lord Krishna, Bhagavad-gita, 4.39)

Knowledge means strength, and strength means victory over our enemies. We have first-hand experience of this from our own life experiences. We may have been initially afraid to learn how to drive a car, but through practice we gained enough knowledge to the point where we can now drive without even being consciously aware of it. Eventually our fear was removed. When starting a new job, we might be afraid that we won't be able to successfully perform our duties. Yet through time and experience, we gain a better understanding of our work requirements, and our fears are removed. Often times our acquired knowledge is so vast, that we gain the confidence to teach others and remove their fears in the process.

Knowledge and experience are the only way to remove our regular mundane worries, but we see that new fears keep popping up. As single adults, we're afraid that we'll never get married and be forced to die alone. After getting married, then we worry about whether the marriage will last or not. After we have children, we spend the rest of our lives worrying about their livelihood. So while knowledge and experience related to material matters may be beneficial, we see that our fears aren't permanently removed.

According to Vedic philosophy, one must gain an understanding of the soul and its relationship with God in order to be completely worry-free. The Sanskrit term *aham brahmasmi*, meaning "I am a spirit soul", is the first step in spiritual understanding. We are all under the misconception that our material bodies represent our identity. Actually, once we die, our material body is destroyed, but our soul is not. The soul represents our real identity, and it is eternal. Lord Krishna says in the Bhagavad-gita,

"For the soul there is never birth nor death. Nor, having once been, does he ever cease to be. He is unborn, eternal, ever-existing, undying and primeval. He is not slain when the body is slain." (Bg 2.20)

Having an understanding of these facts represents a good base from which to start. Such knowledge is categorized as *jnana*, or theoretical. Philosophical understanding is nice, but we have to know to use it before we can really grasp its importance. One may have graduated from a respectable university with a law degree, but one truly doesn't understand the law until they practice it for many years. In the same way, we have to practically apply the transcendental lessons given to us by the Vedic literatures.

Lord Krishna, declared the Supreme Personality of Godhead by the Vedas, incarnated in the Treta Yuga in India as the handsome and pious prince Lord Rama. Rama's father was King Dashratha of Ayodhya, and he had planned to install the Lord as the new king. However, due to a misjudgment on the king's part, the Lord's installation would have to wait, and instead Rama was ordered to live in the forest as a recluse for fourteen years. Sita Devi, Lord Rama's wife, was horrified at the prospect of living without her Lord for such a long period. Rama tried His best to dissuade her from following Him, but He was unsuccessful. As part of Sita's plea to her husband, she let Him know that she would be fearless while in His company.

Women, being the fairer sex, are generally more prone to fearing than men are. This is the way of nature, for men naturally assume the role as protectors of women. Even according to Vedic rules, men are required to provide protection to women at all stages in their life. So how was Sita Devi boldly declaring that she would be fearless? Sita was the incarnation of Goddess Lakshmi, who is the wife of Lord Narayana. Narayana is the presiding deity of the universe, and He is no different than Krishna Himself as declared in the Vedas:

"In the beginning of the creation there was only the Supreme Personality Narayana. There was no Brahma, no Shiva, no fire, no moon, no stars in the sky, no sun. There was only Krishna, who creates all and enjoys all."

Being God's wife, Sita was one hundred percent devoted to Him. Being raised in kingdom of the pious King Janaka of Mithila, Sita had the philosophical understanding of the soul imparted on her during her childhood. Through her marriage to Rama, she gained the practical understanding of this knowledge by serving God personally. Practical understanding is known as *vijnana*, and it comes only through the process of devotional service, or bhakti yoga. *Bhakti* means love and *yoga* means union of the soul with God. So if we love God, then we always stay with Him and He always stays with us.

Practicing bhakti yoga raises us to the *brahma-bhuta* platform of understanding. According to Lord Krishna, our fears are completely removed once we reach this platform:

"One who is thus transcendentally situated at once realizes the Supreme Brahman. He never laments nor desires to have anything; he is equally disposed to every living entity. In that state he attains pure devotional service unto Me." (Bg, 18.54)

The system of bhakti yoga is executed through nine different processes: hearing, chanting, remembering, serving the Lord's lotus feet, worshipping His deity, offering prayers, following His orders, serving as a friend, and completely surrendering everything to Him. Sita Devi, being the perfect devotee and wife of the Lord, actually practiced and perfected *all* nine of these processes. Such a great soul is very rare. For us mere mortals, perfecting even one of these processes will make our lives successful. In this age, Lord Chaitanya has stated that chanting is the easiest and most effective method for transcendental realization. Chanting the maha-mantra, **"Hare Krishna Hare Krishna, Krishna Krishna, Hare Hare, Hare Rama Hare Rama, Rama Rama, Hare Hare"**, is the best weapon in our war against fear.

Perfect Yoga

133

"The hatha-yoga system is meant for controlling the five kinds of air encircling the pure soul by different kinds of sitting postures-not for any material profit, but for liberation of the minute soul from the entanglement of the material atmosphere." (Shrila Prabhupada, Bhavagad-gita, 2.17 Purport)

Yoga has become a very popular phenomenon in the modern age. One can find classes, books, and videos on yoga everywhere. It has become such a profitable business that people are even inventing their own forms of yoga and marketing it to the masses. Though there are many different forms of yoga, today the term is generally associated with the system of hatha-yoga, which involves various sitting postures and breathing exercises.

People generally take to yoga so that they can improve their overall health. Athletes take to it as a means of increasing their stamina and flexibility. That in turn relates to longer careers and greater earnings. Yoga's effectiveness lies in its requirement that one be steady of mind. We see examples of this in our daily lives. If we are concentrated on our particular job or hobby, then we are more likely to be successful at it. Superstar golfer Tiger Woods is known for his impeccable concentration. When on the green, he says that he pictures the ball going into the cup prior to putting. This technique allows him to visualize his putts prior to striking the ball. Being lost in the moment or being in the "zone" as athletes call it, is a wonderful feeling. The mind is always hankering or lamenting, but when concentrated on something, it is at peace.

These activities represent a form of yoga, as it defined today, since the mind is steadily brought under control. However, real yoga actually means linking our consciousness with God. It was a system invented by God and passed down through generations by the great sages of India. It shouldn't be surprising to find out that a system that was intended to bring spiritual benefits will also have accompanying material benefits. The various breathing exercises and sitting postures are all aimed at eliminating the effect of the senses and towards controlling the mind on Vishnu, or God. Gradually over time, the system has degraded into nothing more than a set of gymnastics exercises.

People saw the potential material benefits afforded to yogis, so they jumped on the bandwagon, eliminating God from the picture completely. Many students in the modern day yoga classes are even accustomed to reciting the syllable of *om*, though they have no idea what it really means. Some even go so far as to say that om is just a peaceful sound that helps one in their practice of yoga. From the Bhagavad-gita, we get the true definition:

"O son of Kunti [Arjuna], I am the taste of water, the light of the sun and the moon, the syllable om in the Vedic mantras; I am the sound in ether and ability in man." (Lord Krishna, Bg, 7.8)

Om, which stands for omkara, is the original transcendental sound. It is non-different from Krishna. Therefore all important Vedic rituals begin with this sound.

"...the omkara transcendental sound used in the beginning of every Vedic hymn to address the Supreme Lord also emanates from Him. Because the impersonalists are very much afraid of addressing the Supreme Lord Krishna by His innumerable names, they prefer to vibrate the transcendental sound omkara. But they do not realize that omkara is the sound representation of Krishna." (Shrila Prabhupada, Bg 7.8 Purport)

In this day and age, the hatha-yoga system is very difficult to perform successfully. Lord Krishna describes the strict rules required for success at such a system in the Bhagavad-gita. One is required to live in a secluded place, and completely abstain from sex life.

"Persons learned in the Vedas, who utter omkara and who are great sages in the renounced order, enter into Brahman. Desiring such perfection, one practices celibacy..." (Lord Krishna, Bg 8.11)

With the hustle and bustle in today's society, practicing yoga in such conditions is very impractical. Therefore, Lord Chaitanya, Krishna's incarnation in the Kali Yuga, advised us to simply chant the holy names of God: "**Hare Krishna Hare Krishna, Krishna Krishna, Hare Hare, Hare Rama Hare Rama, Rama Rama Hare Hare**". This process, executed with love and devotion, is known as bhakti-yoga. It is the best form of yoga because it involves the two direct processes of *sravanam* and *kirtanam*, hearing and chanting. By lovingly repeating the Lord's name, we control our speech. At the same time, we purify our hearing as mundane noise is drowned out by the sound of God's names.

By steadily chanting, we raise ourselves to the platform of loving God, which means always thinking of Him. If we're always thinking of Him, then we'll be performing the highest form of yoga. Playing sports, listening to music, or exercising may give some temporary comfort for the mind, but real happiness comes when we focus our mind on God. If we make loving God our number one occupation, then we reap the rewards of the all yoga systems combined.

A Divine Vision

137

"Being installed this day, do you following in the footsteps of your fathers and grandfathers cherish and protect us. With you taking the reins of government, we shall live more happily than we did under your ancestors. We seek not earthly comforts or the highest things in this life, for our only wish is to see Rama installed in the kingdom. There is nothing more pleasing to us than the installation of the highly energetic Rama on the throne." (Citizens of Ayodhya offering benedictions to Rama prior to His installation as king, Valmiki Ramayana, Ayodhya Kand Sec 17)

The king of Ayodhya, Maharaja Dashratha, had announced that his eldest son, Rama, God Himself in human form, would be installed as the new king. On the day of the installation, Lord Rama travelled from His residence to the king's, and the town citizens praised Him as He went by.

One of the first kings ever was Maharaja Ikshvaku. He was highly pious, considered the lord of earth. From him descended a long line of pious kings, of which Dashratha was one. Not having any sons, the king performed a great sacrifice which awarded him four sons, of which Rama was one. Dashratha's favorite son from the outset, Rama was loved and adored by all. The king couldn't wait until the day would come when Rama would succeed him on the throne. One day, after properly consulting the learned brahmanas of the kingdom, Dashratha decided the time was right to crown Rama as his successor.

We can understand from the above referenced verse that the citizens of Ayodhya were highly advanced devotees for they were given the opportunity to directly witness Lord Rama's pastimes. In the modern day governments of the world, leaders of democratic nations are elected to their posts directly by the citizens. A simple majority vote is usually required to win office, meaning that even the most popular of leaders doesn't enjoy universal favorability. In America, polling firms take daily tracking polls of a president's favorability rating. As long as a president is approved of by at least fifty percent of those polled, he is considered to be popular. That still means almost half the population isn't happy with the job the president is doing.

This was not the case during Lord Rama's time. The people knew that the Lord loved them all equally and that He didn't favor any one group over another as leaders do today. They all approved of Him. As a prince following the duties of the kshatriya order, Rama would have to punish people from time to time. Yet even those people couldn't find any faults in Him.

"I do not find any such man in this world, even amongst great enemies, who, forsaken for heinous sins, can cite, even in His absence, any fault of Him." (Lakshmana speaking to Kausalya about Lord Rama, Vm, Ayodhya Kand, Sec 21)

As stated previously, Lord Rama was born into a very auspicious family, which had a great heritage dating back many generations to King Ikshvaku. They were all extremely pious men who were dedicated to dharma, or religiosity. The citizens were well aware of the family history, but still they were the most pleased when Rama was to be installed.

The attitude of the people also represents the highest form of devotion to God. People who turn to God can be classified into one of four categories:

"O best among the Bharatas [Arjuna], four kinds of pious men render devotional service unto Me-the distressed, the desirer of wealth, the inquisitive, and he who is searching for knowledge of the Absolute." (Lord Krishna, Bhagavad-gita 7.16)

Most of us fall into either the first or second category. We ask God for things: "Please take away my pain. God, give us our daily bread.

God, why am I in such distress?" Undoubtedly, it is always beneficial to us anytime we can think of God.. However, true love means wanting more for the person you love than you want for yourself. The citizens of Ayodhya didn't want anything from Lord Rama. Instead they only wished to see Him happy, in the same way that a parent wants more for their children than they want for themselves. The citizens had completely renounced all worldly comforts. Their happiness was tied to God's. Achieving this state of mind means one has perfected their life.

As it turned out, Providence would play its role, and Rama would be denied the kingdom on that day. Banished to the forest by his father, the citizens would have to suffer the pains of separation from the Lord for fourteen years. Fear not, for Rama would triumphantly return and fulfill the wish of his devotees. The lesson we take away from this is that God always hears us. If we truly love Him and always think of Him, then He'll deliver us from any calamity.

Real Heaven

141

"He to whom heaven and hell and liberation are all one – for he beholds but You everywhere armed with bow and arrows – and who is Your servant in thought and word and deed – in his heart, Oh Rama, make Your permanent abode." (Maharishi Valmiki speaking to Lord Rama, Ramacharitamanasa)

The existence of a heaven is a belief shared by almost all religions. As human beings, all we know is what we've witnessed in this life, and heaven represents the great unknown. Many of us eventually realize that this material world is full of miseries. Thus heaven represents our reprieve, a sort of resting place after we have finished our work in this life.

In general, most religions believe in heaven being a permanent residence for those who are good in this life. In Christianity, the belief is that all souls either go to heaven or to hell after this life depending on how they behaved. Hell is believed to be a very distressful place, ruled over by the devil with scorching hot temperatures due to a constant fire. Heaven is just the opposite, a place of complete happiness where there are no miseries. The time of death is referred to as judgment day, where it is decided whether the soul will enter heaven or be condemned to hell. Other religions envision heaven as a place where there is unlimited sense gratification, with beautiful women and an unending supply of sumptuous food.

Vedic philosophy also has its concept of heaven, but it differs slightly from other religions. The Vedas tell us there are indeed heavenly and hellish planets, but residence there is not permanent. Lord Krishna, the Supreme Personality of Godhead, has created the material world with its millions of different planets. He has also deputed highly advanced souls known as demigods to manage the affairs of the material world. The god of death, known as Yamaraja, determines whether a soul will enter heaven or hell after it quits its current body. A person accumulates good and bad karma in their lifetime, and these merits or demerits determine which planet they will travel to after quitting their body. There are many different heavenly planets, each having their unique mode of enjoyment. In the same way, many hellish planets exist where different styles of punishment are handed out. However, these merits or demerits eventually expire and the soul is forced to accept a new body in the material world. Thus, the laws of karma repeat, causing spirit souls to constantly transmigrate from one body to another based on their fruitive work.

When Lord Krishna incarnated as Lord Rama many thousands of years ago in Ayodhya, He was forced into exile by His father, King Dashratha. Being married at the time, the Lord tried to convince His wife, Sita Devi, to remain in the kingdom during His exile period. Sita, however, refused to remain at home and rather insisted on coming along.

"Remaining dedicated to You, O large eyed one, I shall regularly bathe in those ponds and sport with You in full joy. Even if I stay with You for hundreds of thousands of years, I shall not feel any loss. Even residence in the heavenly realm is not preferred by me. O Raghava, even if I live in the heavenly realm, if I am without You, I will not find any pleasure there, O tiger among men." (Sita Devi speaking to Lord Rama, Valmiki Ramayana, Ayodhya Kand, 27.19-21)

In trying to persuade her husband, Sita told Him that she would always remain with Him no matter how long He had to live in the forest. She said that she didn't find living in heaven appealing if He wasn't there with her. In so saying, Sita exhibited the qualities of the perfect devotee of God. The heavenly planets are very nice, but one cannot remain there forever. The enjoyment on those planets is still on the material platform and thus one is forced to accept a material body upon completing his or her stay in heaven. However, there is a spiritual realm known as Krishnaloka and Vaikuntha, that is above all the heavenly planets for it is where Krishna and His various expansions reside. One who goes there never returns to the material world. In the Bhagavad-gita, Lord Krishna says that anyone who thinks of Him at the time of death, never takes birth again.

"And whoever, at the time of death, quits his body, remembering Me alone, at once attains My nature. Of this there is no doubt. Whatever state of being one remembers when he quits his body, that state he will attain without fail." (Bg 8.5-6)

While it is natural for us to want unending happiness, a devotee of the Lord actually rises above this desire. A pure devotee only wants to make God happy, and only thinks in terms of God's interests. Sita Devi taught us that we should strive to think the same way that she did. Material happiness may be nice, but real happiness is *Ramananda*, the bliss that comes through association with Rama, or God. Krishna is the reservoir of pleasure. Life without Him is no life at all. By being constantly engaged in devotional service, one can feel a pleasure that is completely spiritual and above all the effects of karma.

A devotee will gladly go anywhere, heaven or hell, as long as they can worship the Supreme Lord. If we practice lovingly chanting the holy names of the Lord, **"Hare Krishna Hare Krishna, Krishna Krishna, Hare Hare, Hare Rama Hare Rama, Rama Rama, Hare Hare"** then we too can rise above the material platform and book our ticket back home, back to Godhead. Eternal association with God represents true heavenly life.